CREDIT REPAIR

Remove Negative Accounts From Your Credit
Report and Raise Your Credit Score

(Simple Guides to Debt, Credit, and Wealth Book)

Thomas Gomez

Published by Knowledge Icons

Thomas Gomez

All Rights Reserved

Credit Repair: Remove Negative Accounts From Your Credit Report and Raise Your Credit Score (Simple Guides to Debt, Credit, and Wealth Book)

ISBN 978-1-990084-72-0

Legal & Disclaimer

The information contained in this book is not designed to replace or take the place of any form of medicine or professional medical advice. The information in this book has been provided for educational and entertainment purposes only.

The information contained in this book has been compiled from sources deemed reliable, and it is accurate to the best of the Author's knowledge; however, the Author cannot guarantee its accuracy and validity and cannot be held liable for any errors or omissions. Changes are periodically made to this book. You must consult your doctor or get professional medical advice before using any of the suggested remedies, techniques, or information in this book.

TABLE OF CONTENTS

Introduction

We are best known for a unique program called Prosperity Partners Elite. In this program we

teach a group of people (in a simple step-by-step manner) exactly how they can make plenty

of money and gain financial freedom harnessing the power of free classified ads on

Craigslist, Backpage,Facebook & Twitter. Membership is offered strictly by personal

to anyone else. It is for you only.

Meanwhile, on with the task at hand. How To Raise Your Credit Score 100 Points and Gain

$1000's in CA$H Spending Power incidentally, has nothing to do with the PROSPERITY

PARTNERS ELITE or various blogs.This unique system was devised for average people with

below poverty level wages to LEVERAGE CREDIT for more income. The exciting thing about

this is you can START from nothing.

Chapter 1: Understanding The Credit Score: How Does It Work & What Is It Reliant On?

The mistake most people make is that they jump straight into attempting to boost their credit score without doing enough research as to what it really is and what factors come into play when generating this score. This could be a major reason why so many people fail to boost their credit score even when the instructions they follow are as simple as can be. Like is the case with most things, getting an understanding of the credit score before doing anything to change its state will do you a lot of good. This chapter will help you understand what it is and what elements influence its generation.

What Exactly Is A "Credit Score"?

A credit score, first and foremost, is a statistical number. With all statistics and statistical numbers, the end goal is usually to define some degree of value or some "measure of extent". In the case of the credit score, it will define your creditworthiness, which is to say your credit score will play a central role in whether you are allowed credit by businesses or financial institutions, such as banks.

Your credit score will range from 300 to 850. The higher your score is, the more financially trustworthy you are.

The average score range:

Excellent: 750+

Good: 700-749

Fair: 650-699

Poor: 550-649

Bad: 550 and below

Think of your green grocer who constantly allows you to carry items on credit. He does so time and time again because he knows you are good for the money the items cost. Your personal relationship with him, as well as your promptness in paying off owed amounts, has convinced him that your creditworthiness is very positive. As such, he feels no fear at letting you carry items without paying immediately. It is impossible to establish the same personal relationship with, say, a bank, as it has several other million customers to attend to as well. As such, all the bank has to go by is your credit score. This will be their measure of just how reliable you are in paying off debt.

You could be the most reliable and trustworthy person around but if a few bad items, such as late payments or errors that you are in no way responsible of, are negatively affecting your credit score, financial institutions will treat you as one who is unworthy of loans and such kind.

So what is the credit score based on?

What is the credit score based on?

Simply put, it is 100% based on your credit history. Your past actions in how you handle money and repay debts speak volumes on how you are likely to behave in the future with regard to the same. A lender is apt to think, "This fellow has a low credit score. This is quite poor and it shows he cannot be trusted. It makes more sense to refuse to lend him money."

Let me break this down for you so that you can understand it:

FICO (Fair Isaac Corporation) came up with a model that most financial institutions use. There are other scoring systems without a doubt, but the FICO score is by and large the most commonly used.

As such, when you are looking to boost your credit score, or simply keep it high, it is important to ensure your actions go toward influencing the elements that the FICO uses in scoring. Let me give an example:

How do you possess high credit scores?

This is straightforward- you simply maintain a good track record of paying your bills on time. You may not think much on making a late payment- after all, you did pay it off, right? But this will certainly play a part in influencing your score. Especially when you consider that a late payment can make a dent in your credit score for up to 7 years, you may want to think twice on making late payments from now on.

In addition, always make a point of keeping your debt low as this will greatly help your credit score. Lenders and other decision makers use your credit score to make different decisions.

Let me explain this by using lenders:

How will your credit score influence lenders?

Look at this:

If you have a credit score below 640, the lender usually has a name for you- you are a "subprime borrower." That does not sound good now, does it? If the lending institution does not tell you to take a hike and decides to lend to you anyway, it will attach a special interest rate on your "subprime mortgage". It does not take a genius to tell that the interest rate will be higher than that of a conventional mortgage. But why should this happen? If you were to ask, the customer care lady would politely tell you that the institution has to compensate itself for "carrying more risk by the simple act of lending to you." If you think about it, it is as valid an argument as they come. The lending institution may also require that you pay off your debt in a shorter repayment term or that you have a co-signer.

A credit score of 700+ is generally considered good. You will receive lower interest rates, which of course will result in paying less money over the loan's life.

So which factors determine how high or low your credit score is?

Factors That Will Influence Your Credit Score

Payment history: This will account for 35% of your score. It will factor in information about your account payment, with the inclusion of any delinquencies as well as public records in place.

Amounts that are owed: This will account for 30% of your score. Exactly how much do you owe on your accounts? The available credit amount that you are using on different revolving accounts is often weighted heavily.

Length of credit history: This will account for 15% of your score. It points to the period that you have had your accounts open a accounts and the time since you conducted any account activity.

New credit: This will account for 10% of your score. It points to your pursuit of new credit, with the inclusion of credit inquiries as well as the number of recently opened accounts.

Types of credit used: This will account for 10% of your score. It basically points to the mix of accounts you have, such as installment and revolving.

I know you might still be wondering:

Will personal or demographic information influence your score?

If this worries you, let the worry cease right now. It will not affect your score in any way. You could be 21 years old but if your borrowing and paying habits are great and you keep your debt low, your score will be high. It does not matter what race you are, where you live, what income you make and whether you are employed or not. All this is your personal business and the credit score will have nothing to do with it.

Now that you have a basic understanding of what credit score is and what makes the credit score, next, we will start discussing how to improve your credit. We all could use a little better credit rating, right?

Chapter 2: Fico What??

I Know What My FICO Score Is

It's a good idea for someone to obtain their FICO score at least once a year. This is a service that is paid for (the fee isn't expensive), and I do this every year to see where I stand. Each of the three credit bureaus maintains a FICO score for us. I don't usually purchase all three FICO scores at once, and instead purchase a FICO score from a different credit bureau every year. You can do what feels right for you.

A FICO score is a number between 300 – 850. According to myFICO.com, here is a general guideline for how to evaluate your score:

720 – 850 (excellent)

660 – 719 (good)

600 – 659 (fair)

300 – 599 (bad)

If you're FICO score is in the excellent range, congratulations! Keep up the good work! What steps in this book can support you in maintaining your excellent rating?

If you're FICO score is in the good range, then you are also doing well! Keep up the good work! What steps in this book can you take to raise your score to the excellent rating?

If you're FICO score is below the good range, don't despair! There IS hope! It IS possible to raise that score by following some of the steps in this book and being responsible with your spending habits.

Calculating your FICO score is based on the following items from your credit report:

Payment History (approximately 35%)

Amounts Owed (approximately 30%)

Length of Credit History (approximately 15%)

New Credit (approximately 10%)

Types of Credit Used (approximately 10%)

(These percentages are used as general guidelines and each percentage may change depending on an individual's credit situation.)

Some things that may lower a FICO score and credit worthiness are:

Having accounts in collections.

Using all or most of one's credit (for example maxing out credit cards)

Bankruptcies. There are different types of bankruptcies and they can last on someone's credit report for 7-10 depending on which one is filed.

Having several inquiries on one's credit report.

Late or missing payments.

A higher FICO score may let you have access to a higher credit limit for a credit card or a very low interest rate for a car payment, loan, or a home mortgage. Having a low interest rate is a good thing because you save money paying less on interest on your loan. People with lower FICO scores will likely pay higher interest rates and therefore significantly more money for the product that they buy.

Knowing what my FICO score is helps me keep my goal in mind for what I want to improve. Avoiding knowing this number has created anxiety and worry for me in the past.

Chapter 3: Why Your Credit Score Matters

Arguably more important than understanding the history of credit is why your credit score is important. While the introduction of the book discussed how the ability to borrow money from banks and other types of institutions can help you to be able to afford luxury goods like boats and cars, the reality is that other types of lenders also look to your credit history in order to determine how much they will allow you to borrow and at what interest rate. These types of businesses include the auto insurance industry, the home owner's insurance industry, apartment management offices, and mortgage companies. By understanding how your credit score influences areas of your life that goes beyond simply buying goods, it will become clearer why maintaining a satisfactory credit score is important for multiple spending categories. Let's take a look at four reasons why your credit score matters.

Reason 1: Your Credit Score Determines How Much You Pay for Goods

Of course, your credit score is not going to influence how much you pay for a gallon of milk or how much the gas station attendant charges you at the pump, but your credit score will influence how much you pay for big purchases, such as a loan you take out for buying your first car and buying your first house. So far we have only discussed how lenders look at your credit score, but the reality is that insurance companies also examine your credit score in order to see how responsible you are. For example, your credit score can be used by the auto insurance industry as a way to determine how safe you will be on the road. If you don't see your credit card bills as important and you rarely pay them on time, it can be assumed that you might be less likely to be responsible on the highway. With a bad or low credit score, the auto insurance vendor is more likely to assume that there's a chance you'll run that red light at a four-way intersection, resulting in a crash. You spending behavior thus indicates the amount of risk you will cost the insurance company. While we will discuss other reasons why your credit score matters, this reason alone should be enough for you to realize how important your credit score can be.

Reason 2: Your Credit Score Influences Where You Can Live

If you have ever rented an apartment in your lifetime, you know that part of the application process requires your social security number. The apartment complex uses your social security number as a way to access your credit score. Let's say that you want to rent an apartment in a nice part of New York City. You just got a new job, and so you're able to pay for a higher priced apartment. If the leasing office at the apartment complex checks your credit score and finds that your score is low, you might not be eligible to rent the apartment that is your first choice. Being denied the ability to live in an apartment, even when you have the immediate funds available to pay for it, has drastic implications for your life. For example, you will have to live in an apartment where the credit score minimum is lower, meaning that it's likely that the apartment itself won't be as nice because there is more of a chance that the types of people who rent these apartments are less responsible than the ones who are renting the apartments in the nicer area of town. Additionally, factors such as the crime rate will probably be different depending on where you live. The implications for your ability to lease an apartment based on your credit score is a real concern that you should have, especially if you know that your credit is weak.

Additionally, it's doubly important to understand how your credit affects your ability to qualify for mortgage loans if you're looking to buy a house instead of rent an apartment. In the past, the mortgage lending banks made it harder for people with bad credit to attain mortgage loans. The idea was that these people were high risks and more likely to default on their mortgage payments, resulting in bankruptcy and housing foreclosures. However, while this was the consensus for a long time, more recently the banks have become more lenient on who qualifies for obtaining a household mortgage loan. By becoming more lenient, the bank is able to charge more interest against the money that is being borrowed by the aspiring homeowner. The consequences of this decision became known in 2008 at the time of the international economic crisis, which was caused primarily by mistakes that had been made in the housing industry. The lenders became less concerned about whether or not an individual would be able to keep up with a high mortgage payment, and more concerned about lining their wallets. As a borrower, you need to be weary of blindly trusting a bank when it tells you that you are qualified to borrow a high amount of money, especially if you know that your credit history is questionable. If you borrow a lot of money from a mortgage company, the possibility exists that you will not be able to pay back your loan. You could end up bankrupt.

Reason 3: It's Hard to Revive a Bad Credit Score

It takes only one mistake for your credit score to sour. For example, let's say that you don't pay your Comcast television bill for months. Comcast continuously calls you, reminding you to make your payments, but after three months of refusing to pay, they turn off your cable. It's not that you didn't want your cable anymore, it's that you couldn't afford their high rates for those couple of months. Once Comcast turns your cable off, those old bills don't just disappear. Comcast will still require that you pay them for the three months of free cable that you got. Eventually, the possibility exists that the company will hire a collection agency who will hunt you down until you agree to pay Comcast for what you owe them. If you have ever been approached by a collection agency in the past, what you may have not realized that your inability to pay your bills also resulted in a knock on your credit score. When negative factors are transcribed onto your credit score, it can go down by at least one hundred points. This isn't something that can be easily resolved; it can take years to revitalize the mistakes that you made in regards to your credit. Additionally, your credit score will matter far into the future, and each historical account of your score will stay on your credit history for at least seven years. A simple or seemingly innocuous action on your part can be perceived by your credit score to be big and damning. This is why it's important to carefully choose who you're going to be dealing with when you decide to buy a product or service from a company. Some companies are stricter than others. Spend beyond your ability to pay back what you owe, and your credit score could be negatively impacted far into your future.

Reason 4: Bad Credit Has Implications for Your Dating Life

Less tangible but still relevant are the negative factors that bad credit can have on your romantic relationships. Think about it. While it may seem like bad credit will only make you feel guilty, sad, or angry, there can also be an unattended impact on the people you love. Additionally, if you're currently single, it might be harder to find a potential boyfriend or girlfriend is you have a bunch of financial baggage that you're carting around. If you have a good credit score, it's important to be weary of people in your life who might try to pawn their lousy spending habits on you. This reality could manifest itself through the person asking you to burden some of their debt. He or she may even ask you to take some of their debt into your name, if your relationship becomes serious. It's important to establish limits with whomever you're associating with romantically, as well as realize that financial burdens can serve to sour and end relationships. Establish good credit habits in order to curtail this potential issue.

Understanding why your credit matters is the first step in attempting to establish ways to fix, maintain, and grow your credit overtime. If you don't have a sense that your credit is significant in multiple ways, you will be less likely to care about its health. Sometimes, people spend money on their credit cards without being aware of the many ways in which credit is analyzed by multiple companies. Remember, your credit score can influence how much you pay for auto insurance, home insurance, and can influence how high your rent or mortgage payments are. It cannot be overstated that you need to be careful when negotiating with mortgage lenders, and be sure to honestly assess your financial stability before buying a home. While it can take years to fix a bad credit score, it is possible and will be discussed in depth in a later chapter. Lastly, remember that bad finances in general can be bad for your intimate relationships. If you look at a credit score as an indication of how well you will maintain important relationships in your life, it might be easier to recognize how important it is to make your credit score a toppriority.

Chapter 5: Causes That Lead To Bad

Credit

In the previous chapter, we looked at some of the terms that you must thoroughly understand so as to better read your credit report. In this chapter, I will tell you the main reasons that might be causing you to have bad credit.

Remember that these might only be a few of the reasons and there might be more that might be contributing towards your bad credit. If you identify and relate to yours from this list, then it is best that you tackle the issue immediately to better your score at the earliest.

Having too many cards

One of the main reasons for having bad credit is because of having too many credit cards. When you reach your credit limit on a card or owing to fearing a max out, you decide to apply for another and then another and then another one. Ultimately, you will end up having just so many cards that you will not know which one you used to make which large purchase. You will also end up getting a big bill for your cards and not be in a position to pay the debt in full. This debt will keep accumulating and start to stress your credit report out.

Closing cards with credit

The next biggest contributor to your bad credit is you closing out cards that still contain credit. If you do so, then your account balance will remain but your credit limit will be mentioned as 0$. So that will appear like you have maxed out your card limit and it will have a bad impact on your credit score. So without any fault of yours, you will have a bad remark in your report and it will be mentioned that you have maxed out your card even if you have not. And since 30% of your credit score is your debt, this will contribute towards upping that score.

Maxing out credit cards

The next wrong move is for you to max out on your credit cards. By maxing out your limit, it means that you have utilized 100% of your limit and that is not good for your score. It will up your debt ratio by quite a margin and that is not good for your report. Creditors will look at your maxed cards and wonder if you will do the same with theirs. They will not trust you if you show them that you are capable of maxing out your limit on a monthly basis.

Borrowing excessive loans

If you are the kind that borrows a loan for every little thing, then your credit score will be quite low. As was mentioned earlier, a low credit score will be very bad for you as nobody will be willing to give you credit. Even if they do, you will get it at a very high rate, which is not good for you. You might end up having to pay a lot of interest money, which is quite dangerous for your wealth assets. This loan taking might be a habit for you but it will prove to be disastrous for your creditworthiness and cause you to have very bad credit.

Wrong scores

Many times, creditors and credit card companies would have wrongly billed you or added I transactions that you would not have made. That can cause you to have a bad credit score. The creditor might have genuinely made a mistake and caused an error and so, it is important for you to check and thoroughly scan your bills every single time, just to make sure that nothing has been wrongly added. This also applies to the credit bureau and you must check your credit records over and over again to make sure that it is correctly made.

Mortgaging

Not paying up on mortgage or delaying it can be quite bad for your credit. When you do so, your house might get foreclosed and your credit score will be very bad. You will not be able to free your house and might also lose it. You may also have problems in availing mortgages in the future and also have trouble scoring loans and credits. All of it will ultimately cause you to have extremely bad credit.

Declaring bankruptcy

Many times, you might be tempted to declare bankruptcy just to get out of a problem and make it easier for yourself. But filing for bankruptcy will spell doom for your credit score. It will literally go down to 0, which means that you have no credit at all. Nobody will be willing to entertain you in the future out of fear of you defaulting to pay their money. Your bad credit will also make it impossible for you to apply for cards, as they will not be ready to take that risk.

Collections

Many times, creditors will trust a third party to collect the amount that you owe them. This mostly happens with creditors who have had a bad experience with you in the past and do not trust you much. When such a thing happens, it will show badly on your credit report as it will be mentioned that the creditor was tired of trying to make you pay up and has decided to seek outside help to do the job for them. So it is best that you not have your account sent for collections lest you end up with a bad credit score.

Chapter 6: Understand The System

To live to our fullest we must first understand the systems that permeate our lives. Consider the early history of human flight. We've all seen the footage: giant multi-winged contraptions bouncing, whirling, collapsing, occasionally heading over cliffs to their demise. Early inventors had intelligence, dreams and creativity in abundance. They merely lacked a sufficient understanding of the system they were trying to harness: in this case, aeronautics.

Most attempts to improve our financial state are hampered in much the same way: it's not that we lack capability, we simply don't fully understand the system. And our attempts at financial 'flight' often meet similar ends.

Picture today's average borrower in the US:

- Among credit card users the average household credit card debt totals $15,799.

- 27% of households have less than $1,000 in savings.
- 50% of households say they would be unable to cover an unexpected $2,000 expense. (source: creditcards.com)

Another way to put this is that nearly half of Americans are living **paycheck to paycheck,** and many with far more debt than they should carry.

Why?

Many people go through life wholly unaware of the systems of credit and finance and the habits of financial management that lead to greater financial empowerment. As a result, instead of living richly within their means, they spend to the edge of ruin seeking a tabloid life. Rather than setting goals to build a life of intent, they resign themselves to the troubled condition into which they have fallen.

Based on the the statistics, it is clear that many of us don't understand how to prioritize our expenditures or how to use debt. As a whole, we certainly don't know how to manage our finances in a credit friendly way. And without this understanding we leave the condition of our finances to fate.

To begin the process of taking back control: understand the system.

We can take an important lesson here from the world of business banking...

A source of unending frustration to many small business owners is their banks' insistence that their line of credit be used in a certain way. Banks like to see the balances 'revolve'. What this means is that as money comes in it is immediately used to pay down the line. If the business then needs to borrow again, so be it.

What the banks are concerned with is the 'source of repayment'. When a business draws from their line of credit is it typically for one very specific purpose: to cover the period of time between the delivery of goods and services (and the associated costs) and the receipt of payment.

For example: If a business sells a shipment of widgets that costs $25,000 to build but won't get paid for 30 days, that 30 day gap is a perfectly logical space to fill with borrowed funds. The bank is comfortable because it knows exactly where the repayment is coming from. Then, when the payment comes in and is immediately applied to the balance on the line, the balance is said to 'revolve'. Business banking insists on responsible use of credit.

This preoccupation with the source of repayment could completely change the game if it were applied to consumer lending in the same way. But the likelihood that your credit card company is going to suggest that you carefully consider how you're going to pay for your purchases is pretty slim.

Outside of the business world, many of us get ourselves into trouble by believing the lie that is constantly marketed to us: that <u>a credit card exists to purchase things for which we have no money to pay.</u>

This belief is the master key to disaster!

We need to think about credit cards, and any other lines of credit, in the same way a business would. Credit cards should only be used when we know exactly how they are going to be repaid. The source of repayment could be sitting in a bank account you created to save for a specific purchase. It could be a budgeted amount that will arrive with your next paycheck. The money could come from any number of sources, but ultimately the key to borrowing smart is this:

If you don't know where it's coming from, don't spend it!

It's such a simple concept, but clearly one that, culturally, we find extremely hard to put to work in our lives. Nonetheless, it is key to everything that follows. By acknowledging this basic instruction and implementing it in your life you make possible real, substantial and life affirming change.

In addition to learning the appropriate use of credit, we also need to learn the specific terms of our credit accounts and the broader ways we are encouraged to live beyond our means.

What are your interest rates?

How much do you pay in interest as a result?

Are you paying any hidden fees?

What external pressures keep us spending when we shouldn't?

What internal pressures do the same?

What dis-empowering habits do we need to overcome?

Each of these questions is considered in the chapters that follow. Learning the answers is essential to transforming your financial life.

Take Flight!

The challenge before you is not one of capability. It is a challenge of knowledge and commitment. By learning the fundamentals of credit and finance contained within this book, and committing to build new credit friendly habits, you will soon find yourself well positioned to live a life of your own making!

Recommendations to help you **Understand the System:**

1. Study this book to gain a clear understanding of the 'appropriate use of credit'.

2. Learn the terms of your credit accounts. What are your rates? What are your fees? What are your payment terms?

3. Become aware of the pressures, both internal and external, that encourage us to spend when we shouldn't.

4. If you don't know where it's coming from, don't spend it!

Chapter 7: Credit Myths

Whether you like it or not, your credit score is an integral part of your financial life. It is important that you understand what it's all about. Lenders, landlords, insurers, utility companies and employers look at your credit score. It is derived from what's in your credit reports and it ranges between 300 and 850.

Yet, according to recent surveys, more than half of all Americans don't know how these scores are derived, what factors are used to determine the scores, and exactly how the scores are used. For example, if your credit score is 580 you are probably going to pay nearly three percentage points more in a mortgage than someone with a score of 720.

Here's another way to look at it. If you had a $150,000 thirty-year fixed rate mortgage and your credit score qualified you for the best rate, your monthly payments would be about $890, according to FICO scoring.

However, if your credit was poor, it is likely that the mortgage payment would be over $1,200 per month for the same loan. The difference is $3,720 per year, and over the 30 year mortgage you will pay an extra $111,600 for the same house.

With so much depending on your credit score, it's important to understand what it is all about and what are the things that affect it. Unfortunately, people commonly have a lot of misinformation and misunderstanding about their credit score. For your understanding, here are five of the most common credit score myths and the true facts associated with them.

MYTH 1: The major credit bureaus use different formulas to calculate your credit score, which can result in large variations among them.

FACT 1: The three major credit bureaus give their scoring calculations different names. Equifax calls the credit score the "Beacon." Transunion calls it "Empirica." Experian gives it the name "Experian/Fair-Isaac Risk Model." All of these different names for the credit score use essentially the same mathematical formula to come up with the number.

The reason that the credit score you receive from each bureau is different is because the information in your file that is used as the basis for the score varies among the bureaus. For example, the records that one bureau uses may go back farther in time, or a previous lender may have shared its information with only one of the bureaus and not the other two.

Usually the scores are not too far apart from each other. Unless there is a big difference between what each bureau says is your credit score, most lenders will use the one in the middle, or average the three, or possible look at the consolidated FICO score. To make sure your scores are not way out of line, it is important to correct any errors that exist in each of the three credit bureau reports.

MYTH 2: Paying off your debts is all you need to do to immediately repair your credit score.

<u>FACT 2</u>: Your credit score is mostly determined by your past performance (payment history) more than your current amount of debt. It is definitely helpful to pay off your credit cards and settle any outstanding loans, and you should get in the habit of paying you bills on time. But if you have a history of late or missed payments, on-time payments won't remove the damage overnight. It takes time to repair your credit score.

In case your report shows a missed or late payment that was not your fault, such as a payment lost in the mail or misplaced by the lender, you should immediately deal with the credit bureau to correct this error. This is one good reason why you need to keep very accurate records of your payments. For large payments, especially those made to the government for taxes, I strongly recommend sending them by certified mail that can be traced.

<u>MYTH 3</u>: Closing old accounts will boost your credit score.

FACT 3: This is a common misconception. It is not closing accounts that affect your credit score, it's opening them. Closing accounts will never help your score and may actually hurt it. Yes, having too many accounts can hurt your score, but once the accounts are open, the damage has already been done. Shutting the account doesn't repair it but can, instead, make things worse.

Your credit score is affected by the difference between the credit that is available to you and the credit that is being used. Shutting down accounts reduces the total amount of credit available and when compared with how much credit you can now use, your actual credit balances become a larger percentage of the new available credit. This hurts your score.

The credit bureaus also look at the length of your credit history as a factor in determining your score. Shutting down older accounts removes old history, which can make your credit history look younger than it actually is. This can also hurt your score.

As a general rule you should not close accounts unless a lender specifically asks you to do so as a condition for giving you a loan or unless the old account is very costly to maintain. The best thing you can do is just pay down your existing credit card debt. That will definitely improve your credit score.

MYTH 4: Shopping around for a loan will hurt your credit score.

FACT 4: When a lender makes an inquiry about your credit, your score might drop up to five points. Some borrowers think that if they shop around to a number of different lenders that each lender's inquiry will generate another reduction in the credit score. This is not the case. For credit score purposes, multiple inquires for a loan are treated as a single inquiry, as long as they happen within a 45 day period. So it is prudent to do your rate shopping within this 45 day window.

<u>MYTH 5</u>: Companies can fix your credit score for a fee.

<u>FACT 5</u>: If the credit bureaus have accurate information – which they usually do – there is nothing that can be done to "instantly" improve your score. If you have a history of not handling your debts well in the past, the only way to improve your credit score is to show that you can manage you debts in the future. This will take time. Companies that "guarantee" they can improve your score are probably scamming you.

As discussed earlier, if there are errors in your file, you can contact the bureaus yourself. You do not need to pay someone else to do for you. Each of the major credit bureaus has a website (see the appendix), which clearly explains what you need to do to correct an error. It's true that you can hire companies to do this for you, but you will be paying them a lot of money for very little actual work.

In summary, the best ways to improve your credit score are:

·Pay down your debt;

·Pay your bills on time;

·Correct existing errors on your credit reports;

·Apply for credit infrequently.

Chapter 8: Scores Calculated

The score calculation is separated into 5 different sections. Each of these sections accounts for a specific percentage of your score.

1) The largest percentage of your score (35%) is based on your payment history. This makes perfect sense since a good way to determine if you will pay future bills on time is to confirm that you have made your past payments on time. Collection accounts, charge-offs, judgments, and bankruptcies are also a part of this section. Negative history will lower your credit score.

Will all late payments, and other negative information, affect your score equally? No. The more recent the negative information is, the harder it will hit your score. A thirty day late on your credit card last month is worth a lot more points, reduced from your score, than a thirty day late that happened 18 months ago. Don't forget that each negative item on your credit will also be calculated differently depending on who is checking your credit report and the scoring model they are using.

2) The next item that affects your score is the percentage of usage (30%). What do I mean? Lenders want to know whether you control your credit or whether your credit controls you. If bank X gives you a credit card with a $ 1,000 limit, will you spend it all or will you spend a small portion? There is a golden rule that applies here:

"Lenders only give credit to those that do not need it"

It's obviously not as simple as that, but it is a good rule, although many times unfair. Many people only apply for credit when they need it. If your car broke down and the repairs are going to cost $ 2,000, you may go to the bank and ask for a credit card with a limit of $ 2,000. If that were your only credit card, you have now become a risky borrower. Does it make sense that someone who limits what he borrows should be considered riskier than someone who has 10 credit cards? Possibly not. But the banks are looking for self-control. If I give you a credit card with a $ 5,000 limit can you control yourself to only spend $ 1,000? That is what they are looking at.

Joe has 2 credit cards, with a total limit of $ 5,000, and he owes $ 4,500. Mary has 10 credit cards, with a total limit of $ 20,000, and she owes $ 4,500. Which is a riskier borrower for future lenders? They both owe the same amount. But Mary could have spent a lot more but did not. Joe may be a very conscientious customer, but there is no way for the banks to know this. According to his record, Joe spends as much as he can.

This portion of your credit score does not affect all of your credit. This section is limited to your revolving accounts.

What are revolving accounts?

Open accounts are revolving or installment.

An installment account is one where:

a) the amount lent is set at the beginning

b) you use the full amount

c) is set for a fixed amount of payments

d) with fixed payments or a written schedule of future payments.

An installment account is closed once you pay it off and you cannot reuse the amount of the principal that you have paid off. Examples of installment loans are car loans, home loans (except lines of credit), personal loans, student loans.

A revolving account is one where you can reuse the credit as you pay the balance down or off. If you pay off a revolving account the account is not closed. Payments are based on what you owed the previous month instead of being a fixed amount. Examples of revolving accounts are credit cards, store credit cards, gas cards.

Why does the usage calculation not affect installment accounts?

Installment accounts, by definition, start off with you using 100% of the loan. When you buy a car for $ 20,000 and put $ 10,000 down, your loan is for the other $ 10,000. Because installment loans are defined by the fact that you will use 100% of it, they are not used to calculate the usage ratios.

The higher your usage percentage of your revolving accounts, the lower your credit score. If you go over your limit, on your revolving accounts, then your score really takes a big hit. This percentage is calculated for each individual revolving account and as a group.

3) The next highest portion of your credit score deals with the age of your accounts. This will be 15 % of your score. The scoring system will average the age of all of your accounts. The older your history, the better your score.

Sounds simple, right? It is not that simple.

There are several things to consider here.

First of all, the score will consider accounts whether they are closed or not. But if you close the account then it will only remain on your credit report for 10 years, so if you close an old account then you are limiting how old your accounts can be. Also, if you close old credit card accounts then you are reducing your total borrowing limits which will in turn increase the percentage of your limits that you are using (affects the "percentage of use").

Secondly, the system will consider how long the account was in use. If you opened an account 8 years ago and closed it within 6 months of opening it, that account is a 6-month account and not 8 years' worth of credit history.

Which is better? Joe opens a credit card account 7 years ago then closes it a year later OR Mary opens a credit card account 2 years ago and is still using it? Joe will be scored as having 12 months' worth of credit history while Mary will be scored as having 24 months. Mary will have a higher score. What could have Joe done differently? Joe could have left that account opened and used it once a year to pay for lunch. Joe would now have 84 months of credit history and a higher credit score.

My oldest credit card is 29 years old and still ticking. The limit is too low to really be of any major use, but it pays for lunch twice a year and then I pay it off the following month. The average age of my accounts is 6 years and two months. Does my 29-year-old card help my score? You bet it does. Without my oldest card the average age of my credit would drop to 3 years. I pay $ 12 a year to maintain this card and it is well worth it.

4) Account mix is also a part of your credit score. It will be 10% of the score. Account mix means that the scoring system is looking to see what type of credit you have. Do you have only credit cards (revolving) or do you have a home loan (installment), car loan (installment), 2 credit cards (revolving) and a gas card (revolving)? The more diversity in types of credit, the higher your credit score can go.

But what if you don't own a home and your car is paid off? What can you do to have diversity?

One option is to consolidate your credit cards with a personal loan. The personal loan will be an installment loan with fixed payments for a fixed period of time. But remember, that unlike a credit card, a personal loan cannot be reused once paid off so do not pay it off early when possible. **You are trying to get diversity but also a long time of use**. Get a three-year term on the personal loan and pay it as agreed. Even if the amount of the personal loan is small (ex: $ 1,000 personal loan), the idea is to get a mixture of types of accounts not the size of the account. Let me clarify one thing, the personal loan must be from a bank, credit union, or an entity that reports to the bureaus. A personal loan from Uncle John will not help. Also, try and stay away from loans given by last resort type of lenders. A payday loan is an installment account but does not look good on your credit report.

5) The final part of your score comes from inquiries. Inquiries will make up for 10% of your score.

An inquiry occurs when someone checks your credit report. There are two types of inquiries, soft and hard.

A soft inquiry occurs when an employer checks your credit for employment purposes, an insurance company checks your credit for insurance purposes, an existing lender checks to see if you qualify for an increase in your credit limit, etc. So a soft inquiry is not for the purpose of issuing you a new credit account in the future. A soft inquiry will not be shown to other creditors and do not affect your credit score. Only you will be able to see it on your credit profile.

A hard inquiry means that you have applied for a new credit account. These inquiries are viewable by anyone checking your credit report and do affect your credit score. Inquiries will remain on your credit profile for 2 years.

Why would a hard inquiry affect your score? Remember the golden rule we spoke about before;

"Lenders only give credit to those that do not need it"

Well, the golden rule applies here also. Every time you apply for credit your score is lowered. One inquiry may drop your score by 2-3 points. Ten inquiries, within a short period of time, may drop your score by 100 points. Why? The more inquiries you have, the more a lender will think you need credit.

a) Too many inquiries and they will believe that you are desperate for credit,

b) If you are desperate then there is a financial hardship,

c) if there is a financial hardship then you are a risky borrower,

d) Lenders do not like risk

As always, time is your friend. Inquiries will disappear in 2 years. If you need to open a credit account then apply to two or three on the same day if possible, then wait for 6 to 12 months before applying for anymore.

There are a few exceptions to this rule. If you are shopping for a big ticket item such as a home loan or car loan then all inquiries that pertain to this shopping, that are done within two weeks of each other, will be counted as one inquiry. The problem happens when the lender does not classify their inquiry correctly. For example, you go to your local bank shopping for a home loan and the agent runs your report using their "credit card" subscriber number. Companies that do more than one type of loan usually have different accounts from which to run your credit report for each type of loan. Existing customers being checked for increases in credit limits (soft inquiries) will have their credit checked using one system while someone applying for a car loan will be run using a different system. As long as your lender uses the correct system you should be fine. Ask your lender if their system is being used for only your purpose.

Based on this information we can see that those with excellent payment history, that is aged, with many different types of credit, low balances compared to their limits and no inquiries will have the highest scores.

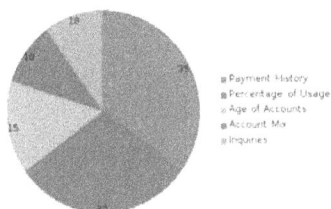

Chapter 9: Factors Affecting Your Score.

There are six factors that have the most bearing on your credit score which means it will behoove you to keep an eye on all of them if you hope to retain a score as close to 850 as possible.

Credit card utilization: Your credit card utilization rate is how much credit you have available compared to how much you are currently using at any one time. It can be determined by simply dividing your credit card balances by the total limits of all of your credit cards. As such, it is beneficial to apply for a number of credit cards, even if you don't ever intend on using them. It is important to keep in mind that this amount is not calculated based on the balance that is on any one card which means you don't need to worry about maintaining a balance and rolling it over from month to month. It is always a better idea to pay off any credit card purchases as the end of the month instead.

On-time payments: Paying your bills on time is one of the easiest ways to ensure you maintain a healthy credit rating. It is weighted very heavily when it comes to influencing your credit card score which means that if you miss a few payments your score is very likely to suffer as a result.

Derogatory marks: Derogatory marks on your credit score include liens, foreclosures, bankruptcies and accounts that are in collections. Each of these will affect your credit rating significantly, with bankruptcies and foreclosures being the most serious. Derogatory marks will stay on your record for up to ten years and, assuming they are accurate, there is little you can do about removing them early. The average amount a derogatory mark will decrease your credit is 50 points.

The monetary amount that lead to the derogatory mark doesn't matter when it comes to your credit rating which means that have a single dollar sent to collections will still ding your credit 50 points. The date of the derogatory mark does matter, however, and it is based on when the negative action took place, not when it occurred. For example, if you defaulted on a debt in 2012 but the account wasn't sent to collections until 2017 then it will be listed as a recent derogatory mark and the seven-year timeframe will start in 2017, not 2012. Additionally, it is important to keep in mind that the derogatory mark will stay on your record regardless of whether or not you have since paid off the outstanding lien or collection amount.

Credit line age: The average age of your lines of credit simply refers to how long you have been building credit for. Lenders like to see that you have a long history of successfully managing credit as it makes it easier to determine if you are a risky investment or not. The longer your credit history, the more likely it is that you have been able to successfully manage your credit. As such, it is never a good idea to close out old credit card accounts, even if you don't use them anymore. Not only will this decrease your total amount of available credit, it will shrink your credit line age average as well. This doesn't just apply to credit cards but also to personal loans, student loans, auto loans and mortgages as well.

Number of accounts: As a general rule, the more lines of credit you have, the higher your credit score will be as it shows you have been given credit by more lenders. Ideally you will want to have a mix of installment and revolving credit lines for the best results. This doesn't mean you will want to go out and open as many credit cards as possible, however, as this factor weighs less heavily on your score than most.

<u>Number of hard credit inquiries</u>: Each time a lender checks your credit score for things like a mortgage, credit card, personal or business loan, student loan or auto loan, it will negatively affect your credit score by a few points. This effect typically wears off after a few months as long as you don't make a habit of promoting these types of checks. The effect is cumulative, however, and having multiple hard credit inquiries in a short period of time is not recommended.

How to get lender offers.

A vast majority of lenders don't have offers that are clearly defined up front, instead they have a general loan package that can be tweaked based on the situation individuals who come to them find themselves in. With this in mind, it becomes apparent why it is so important to seek out multiple offers before making a decision.

Depending on your FICO score, lenders may be more than happy to compete for your business. This fact, coupled with the lack of predetermined rates means that you can easily improve your results by shopping around and then singling out lenders who almost have the rates you are looking for and then telling them that you can get a better deal elsewhere.

To maximize this strategy, you are going to want to make a list of the features you are absolutely going to need to be happy with a given loan and then call each lender you have already talked to and go down the list point by point. If you come across a lender who has an approach that appeals to you, let the other lenders know about it and see what they can do to either match or beat it. They know they are in a competitive business and if you are willing to force their hand they will show you just how much they want your business.

Preapproved offers: If you took advantage of OptOutPrescreen.com to limit soft inquiries on your credit report and are planning on looking for lenders anytime soon then you may want to reconsider and opt back in, at least for the relatively near future. If you have not opted out of the system, and your credit isn't terrible, then putting in an application with one lender will likely trigger a barrage of competing offers from other lenders as creditors will happily provide your information to anyone and everyone who is interested in selling you on their services.

While this can be annoying in some cases, if you are looking for the best lender possible then it could be just what you need to pit several lenders against one another. Prescreened offers can make it easier for you to compare relative costs or special offers as long as you do your due diligence with each and ensure that you aren't being hornswoggled by smoke and mirrors.

Ensure you have a loan estimate document: The loan estimate document was created by the Consumer Financial Protection Bureau to make it easier for borrowers to compare the various costs associated with individual loans and lenders. Its job is to standardize and simplify the way that lenders expose their fees so that you aren't comparing apples to oranges. The loan estimate document can be downloaded from ConsumerFinance.gov.

In addition to make it easier to compare various potential loans, it makes it easy to be aware of the various fees that are sure to pile up along the way, even with the most apparently straightforward of loans. It also breaks down costs in a way that anyone can understand without the help of a CPA. It includes all sorts of useful information including estimated monthly payments, prepayment penalties and the interest rate of the various loans in question.

Lock in the best rate: Once you have done the work of comparing the various options available to you, the next thing you are going to want to do is to ensure that the best option doesn't change while you are making all of the relevant arrangements. To ensure this is the case you are going to want to ask the lender for a written rate lock or lock-in. This is a written and legally binding guarantee that the lender will give you the interest rate you discussed for the price you discussed for a set period of time. It protects you from interest rate increases that may occur while your loan is being processed. It is important to keep in mind that some lenders will charge for a lock-in while others will not it all depends on the individual lender.

Chapter 10: How To Fix Your Bad Credit: A Step-By-Step Guide To Help Change Your Credit Sharply

Being able to fix your bad credit always seems like a wonderful dream because to many it seems to be impossible! You can at times find you want to improve your credit but you simply just do not know where you should start! It can in fact be all too easy to say you want to change your credit but fail to do anything about it.

So, where should you start? Is it even possible to fix your bad credit?

Well, to be honest, yes! Yes, it is possible to fix your bad credit but starting it can often get you stumped but don't panic, because the following is a step by step guide to help you get started in changing your credit.

This is NOT a short fix; it takes time to fix your credit! Usually it takes at least six months before you see any kind of change, but more so a year and you WILL see change for the better.

1. Check Your Credit Report

First of all, you do need to check your credit report carefully! You need to go over every little thing that is contained on your report. You do not want to miss a thing so check carefully and go over it a good few times. You will hear this over and over and over again but it is a good starting point in helping you to fix your credit. Just Do It!

2.Find Errors Within Your Credit Report

Next, you need to find all of those errors within your credit report and fix them. If you make a mistake in failing to make one payment, that is your own fault but do not get caught out by someone else's mistake. If you find any mistake, you need to take note of each and every error and put it into dispute.

3.Disputing Your Errors

Now, to be honest, if you dispute what you think are errors, it could go a long way in helping you to fix some parts of your credit. Not all disputes will be taken into account however but if you do find some incorrect errors there, you should see to get them fixed so that you have accurate information on your credit report.

4.Missed Payments – Catch Up With Them

If you find that there are debts that you are lacking behind payment on or have in fact missed payment on several occasions, you need to catch up with them now! You absolutely need to catch up with any payments you may have missed so that your payment history will be greatly improved.

5.Get Reduced Payments

To be honest, some payments can be quite expensive. However, if you contact your creditors or lenders and ask them to lower the payments each month, it could help you to repay the debt. Remember, lenders want their money even if it means waiting a few more months to get the full amount back. However, they still get their money, so they will be happy.

Call the lender and ask to lower the repayments. This can be great for you and your credit because it helps you to build a good period of repayment history. As long as you pay the loans back, you can improve on your credit greatly.

This is a very frustrating step, DO NOT GIVE UP!! You might be on phone all day long. I like to think of it as negotiating or trying to get the best price for an item. Every phone call you make could save you hundreds of dollars. Remember that. The money you save on this bill could pay off another bill and so on.

6.Don't Struggle With Repayments, Call A Credit Agency

Just say you are at a very bad position with your finances and you do not have the money to repay all debts, you can consult a credit agency. Many agencies out there can help consolidate all of your debts into one monthly repayment price.

This cannot only help you to get rid of your debt but can also make your payments lower and more affordable.

(I DO NOT indorse this, when you can do this yourself in step 5, why pay someone else the money you do not have! However, if you truly do not have the time to deal with all the phone calls and such it is an option.)

7. Pay Each Bill And Debt On Time Every Month

A vital part in ensuring your credit improves is to make each and every month's payments on time. Do not miss out any utility bills and remember your rent and every other cost you pay out.

If you keep making each payment, you are going to find that you can build a good period of repayment history. This all goes into improving your credit score, and to help ensure you do not miss any payments, set up a standing order. This is when the payments are automatically taken from your bank and paid to each company when payment is due.

Though, if you are choosing to automatically pay the companies, check your statements each month. You do not want to overpay especially if you have other bills to worry about. You still need to live each month so ensure the right amount is taken out each time.

8.You Can Get A Late Payment Removed From Your Credit

If you have made a few late payments in the past, you may be able to get those removed from your credit report. Depending on how good your relationship with a company may be and how good your custom is, they may be willing to remove a late payment notice from your credit.

If you do want to try this, why not contact the company in writing and ask if it would be possible. Removing even one late payment can be a great way to help improve your credit altogether. What is more, if you get one late payment removed from every company you have dealt with, it will all count towards a better credit score.

9.Try A Secured Credit Card

When you hear credit card, you do tend to panic a little because you instantly think it means taking on a credit card. However, a secured credit card works a little differently from a normal credit card.

For a start, you have to put money into your account into order to use this, which means you do not spend any more than you can afford and you do not have a bill at the end of the month! However, this can be a great way to start building your credit. Remember, credit allows you to build your credit, which might sound strange but it's true.

That is why you need to try to establish a good form of credit. However, a secured credit card can be a great option if you can use it correctly.

10. Upgrade To An Unsecured Card

After you have made a few good constant months of payments with a secured card, you could try an unsecured card. This can be a way to up your credit though you do not necessarily need to choose a credit card, but rather a store card.

Having a department store card – just one – can be a fantastic way to up your credit. However, you do still need to make every payment each month on time in order to have a good period of payment history.

11. You Can Try A Credit Card

You could go for a normal credit card to help boost your credit. Though, do not try to use several credit cards at once. Stick to one and build small amounts on this so that you can repay each month. Even if it is only fifty dollars worth of things each month, make sure you make each payment because it can go a long way to helping your credit. (At least the minimum payment, but do not get caught in that cycle either though. Pay off as soon as possible when you can!)

12. Don't Close A Credit Card

If you have old credit cards but haven't used them in a very long time, try to avoid having them close. Even though you might not want to use all three of your cards, you do not need to overspend on these.

You can easily put small charges on each to keep the accounts open. At the end of the month, pay the balance off and do the same for the next month. Of course, you do not need to spend for the sake of keeping the account open, put a purchase on the cards that you normally purchase. It can be gas for your car, a meal at a restaurant or just a sweater at a local store. Small is the key here, what you can afford!

13.Keep New Loan Applications Short And Sweet

Searching for a loan for months is never a good thing. If you really need to choose a loan, try to find one within a week or two. Do not have several applicants running at the one time because it can damage your credit. Instead, choose one and stick with one that you know that you can be qualified.

14.Don't Co-Sign For Others While Trying To Fix Your Credit

While co-signing for a new car for your boyfriend or friend may seem nice, it may damage your credit. You cannot afford to have a co-sign loan on your credit because it makes you responsible for it and if that loan is not paid, you are responsible for it. That means you are the one who gets the bad credit!

15.Build Your Credit

Fixing bad credit can be simple but only if you are able to establish new and good credit. Yes, you do need to take care of bad credit but you also need to ensure you establish new credit as well.

Chapter 11: Understanding Your Credit Score & Meaning

A credit score is a number that mirrors your entire credit portfolio, performance and discipline in a specific time frame. It is primarily meant for lenders who evaluate loan applications. Before, it took lenders weeks or months to determine your capacity to pay loan and grant your application. Sometimes, you end up getting disqualified. With credit scores, lenders become faster, more efficient and most importantly adjust their loan offer to you based on your score.

An example of a credit score is the FICO score in the United States. The Fair Isaac Corporation has been using math and other statistics to determine the US citizens' credit score since 1956. Through the FICO score, both client and lenders enjoy an efficient, unbiased and safe lending environment.

Credit scores are usually three digit figures starting from 300 to 850. The higher the score is the better is your credit performance. Below is the scale with their corresponding rating:

1.300 to 550, poor credit

2. 550 to 620, subprime credit

3. 620 to 680, acceptable credit

4. 680 to 740, good credit

5. 740 to 850, excellent credit

Less than 2% of the population has 499 scores, 5% have 549 scores, 8% have 599 scores, 12% have 649 scores and 15% have 650 to 699 scores. The bulk of the population has 749 scores with 18%, 799 scores with 27% and 850 scores with 13%. This shows that the scores are approximately half of the population belong to the lower scores and the other half on the higher scores.

Aside from the population, age also shows a pattern in the credits score. Most 18 to 24 year olds have 638, 25 to 34 with 652,

35 to 44 with 659, 45 to 54 with 685 and 55 and above have 724.

It is difficult or almost impossible to recommend a good credit score. This is because banks and lending institutions are more than willing to serve even those with low credit scores. The only but important difference between those with high and low scores is the interest rate. As a rule, the lower your score is, the higher your interest rate will be. The higher your score is, the lower the interest rate. This rule is applicable to major loan instruments, such as housing and car loans and credit cards.

For example, if you apply for a standard $160,000 mortgage in a 30 year term, the lender will offer you around 9.5% interest rate if you have a poor credit score. This amounts to $259,000 in total payments. On the other hand, if you have an excellent credit score, your interest rate will be offered at around 3.9%. Your total interest payment will be around $89,000.

If you apply for a standard car loan of $25,000 in a 5 year term, the lender will offer you 18.9% or around $13,000 in interest payments if you have a poor credit score. If you have an excellent credit score, your interest rate will be at 5.1% or around $3,500 total interest payments.

This shows how important credit scores are in your financial transactions. They could mean hundreds of thousands of dollars in difference and savings. It is equally important to manage your scores well and especially if you plan to apply for a new loan. Some banks and financial institutions, depending on their risk appetite, may be willing to approve your loan at your expense, in the form of higher interest. Other companies may even offer you pre-approved loans with low interest rates because of your excellent scores.

If you have a poor credit score, there is a huge probability that you will be denied in all your loan applications. Only bankrupt individuals and those with more than 75% delinquency rates belong to this category.

If you have a subprime score, there is a small chance that your loan applications will be granted. However, the terms will really be unfavorable to you. Expect high interest and penalty rates. It is best to postpone the application until you improve your score.

If you have an acceptable score, you will have better chances on your application. However, it will still not be on the best rates.Only few individuals with good scores are denied on their application.

It is almost a guarantee that your loan will be granted in this score. You are a guaranteed a loan and best interest rates if you have an excellent credit score. Take note that just by reaching the minimum 74o threshold, you are part of the excellent score category and you can already enjoy the privileges of those with 741 or extra points in their credit score.

However, it is also best to try to aim for higher scores beyond 741. This is because the extra points may be used as a buffer in case your credit reports become unfavorable. When the reports lower your credit score, the decrease will not be as much because you have points in reserve.

Note that the score may be standard but lenders will have their own criteria for granting a loan. You may have a high score but a lender may disapprove you because of other factors outside your credit score. For example, banks always factor in not only your credit but also your income.

The credit score is calculated based on your portfolio of loans and your performance on paying these loans. Each criterion does not have equal value or each has its own weight in the final credit score. There are generally five categories that form the computation of your credit score:

1. Payment history
2. Principal amount
3. Loan term or length
4. Credit types
5. New credit

Payment history, this has the largest weight in your credit score. It amounts to

35% of the total. This criterion depends on your payment of your loans. The more you pay on time, the better the score will be. Take note that if you have made one or two late payments, these instances do not automatically reduce your score in this category. Most of the time, few late instances are negligible compared to the overall payment history. The more punctual you are on payment, the higher the score is.

Principal amount, this has the second largest weight in your credit score. It amounts to 30% of the total. This score depends on how close you are to reaching the credit limit of your account. Often called maxing out, for example the balance of your credit card is only a few dollars shy from its maximum credit limit. The closer you are to the limit, the lower the score is.

Loan term, this criterion amounts to 15% of the total credit score. This refers to the length of time that you have held the account. For example, you have been subscribing to the credit card account for more than 5 years or you have been paying your monthly installments for a 10 year long term loan. The longer you have an active account, the higher the score is.

Credit types amount to 10% of the total credit score. This refers to the portfolio of accounts that you have. For example, you may have several credit cards, loans for various purposes, mortgages and retail accounts. You may have these accounts in either a bank or a financial institution. The more diverse your portfolio is, the higher the score is.

New credit amounts to 10% of the total credit score. This refers to any pending application or inquiries you have made for new loans. The more inquiries you have, the lower the score is.

Chapter 12: Raise Your Credit Score

Quickly

Raising your credit score can be done in many different ways. The ideas presented below are by no means the only way to boost your score but can be considered if you are interested in a quick boost. Achieving a score over 700 can be done rather quickly but it is up to you to maintain it. We will touch on maintenance in a later section.

The quickest and most efficient way to raise your score is through Revolving Credit (ex. Credit Cards). This is a very powerful part of your score and can actually account for 100 points or more.

First, you need to obtain an updated copy of your credit report. There are several free websites that are available, but I am a true believer that you get what you pay for. Whenever obtaining a copy of your report, weather it is free or not, you need to make sure that you are receiving your

FICO score. This is the score that lenders are going to consider. If you don't have access to the Internet, or are not comfortable obtaining one online you can also call or write all 3 Bureaus (Transunion, Experian, Equifax) to obtain a copy by mail. Here is the contact information:

Equifax800-685-1111 www.equifax.com

Po Box 740241, Atlanta, GA, 30374

Experian888-397-3742www.experian.com

Po Box 2002, Allen, TX, 75013

Transunion800-916-8800 www.transunion.com

Po Box 1000, Chester, PA, 19022

STOP NOW AND OBTAIN YOUR CREDIT REPORT

If you have NO Revolving Credit then you have not tapped into 100 points of your score.

For Example- You currently have a 550 credit score with no revolving credit established. Open one revolving account and generally, within 30 days, you will see an immediate 60-100 point boost to your score.

With revolving credit, all accounts are rolled into one in the eyes of the scoring system. The amount of points you gain depends on the balances of the accounts. Therefore, being that it is based off the balance, it does not matter if you have 1 revolving account or 10 accounts.

For matter of understanding, I am going to explain this two different ways. First, if you have <u>no</u> revolving credit established and, second, if you already have revolving lines in place.

No Revolving Credit Established

<u>*STEP 1</u> - you need to apply for a Credit Card. Or if your score is extremely low you can apply for a Secured Credit Card which is guaranteed approval. This can be done at most any bank or online through different companies. With Secured Credit Cards there is No Credit Check. They will ask you for your Social Security Number because they are going to report to the Credit Bureaus on your behalf. It is similar

to a prepaid Credit Card. You give the creditor the money to provide you with the line of credit. You are securing the line of Credit with your own money. In return, the creditor will report to the Credit Bureau(s) that you have opened an account with them and your payment history.

*When trying to decide <u>where</u> you are going to obtain this credit line it is important to make sure that the creditor reports to <u>all</u> 3 major Credit Bureaus. If they do not, this could defeat your purpose. If they only report to one Bureau then you will be drastically building only one credit score. The goal is to boost all 3 scores. Any time you apply for credit the creditor could look at any one score or all three.

*<u>STEP 2</u> - Most companies will charge you a set up fee. Once you have received your card, immediately pay the balance down to $15 owing. If you are lucky enough to find a company that has not charged you a set up fee, then charge exactly $15 onto

the credit card. Let the $15 balance post to your credit report. This will generally happen within 14-30 days.

*Once the $15 balance has posted to the credit report you will see a drastic increase to your score. **Note – just because the balance post to your credit card company does not mean it has post to the credit bureau. That is why it is important to monitor your credit report. To maximize the last few points of this step, pay the balance to zero. This will post on the next reporting cycle for that company. At this point you should have increased your credit score close to 100 points in as little as 30-60 days.

The next section has very important information. If this is your first time dealing with revolving credit it is pertinent that you keep reading.

Revolving Credit Established on Credit Report

It is important, once you have revolving credit, for you to understand how to

89

calculate your credit score increase from percentages to points. Here is the formula:

Total Balances of all Cards ¸ Total Limits of all Cards=

Percentage of capacity, which is equal to 1 pt per 1%

Example:

LimitBalance

Card 1 500.00 250.00

Card 2 300.00 125.00

Total800.00 375.00

(375.00 ¸ 800.00) = 0.46875 or equal to 47% capacity

47% capacity = 47 pts if you pay the balance down to Zero

Note: It is important to know that your credit card company is reporting the <u>limit</u> of the card to the bureaus. If they are reporting the high credit amount it could alter your results.

This is a quick and easy way to raise your credit score right before a major purchase. However, for the best long-term results it is important to keep your balances below 25% of your limit.

Also, it is necessary for you to use the lines of credit every few months so that activity will be reported to the bureaus. Charge the minimum of $15.00 and then pay it off as soon as your bill arrives. This is important because if the card is inactive (no charges or payoffs) in the last few months, then the Scoring system will not recognize the account and it will be unable to add additional points in the payment history section of your credit score.

Remember this one account will help you to tap into all aspects of how you are scored. Your immediate boost will come from the amounts owed section.

Chapter 13: How To Increase Your Credit

Limit

Now that we have covered some of the good and bad reasons for increasing your credit limit, let's look at how you might actually get it done.

– Call the credit card company – This should be obvious, but you will have to make the first move and give them a call to ask for an increased credit limit. While the credit card company may occasionally give you an increase without you asking, most likely, you will have to take the initiative. Some companies may have online forms for this, but the easiest way is just to give them a quick call.

– Have a good reason – This goes hand in hand with the first section, but having a good reason ready for why you are asking for this, because they will ask. The last time I did it, I was going to be going on vacation a few months later, so I told them I needed the higher limit for that. Have a good reason, even if it is that you want to improve your credit score. Again, if you are desperate, they will know.

– Don't ask too soon – If you have just opened the card within the past few months, it may be too soon. It is best to wait at least six months before you inquire about an increase. Six months seems to be the rule of thumb for this. You may be able to increase it earlier if you are just using the card for basic errands (such as getting groceries), because the lender may then see you as less of a credit risk. However, I would still wait.

– Don't ask for too much – This one is obvious... if you ask for too much and get declined, obviously you have missed your chance. But if you ask for too low of an amount, you might be turning down extra credit that you could have had. It is an obvious catch-22. A good rule of thumb is that you should ask for around 10-25% of your current credit limit.

– Make sure you pay your bills on time – It almost goes without saying that if you are consistently paying your bill late, the creditor will be less likely to increase your limit. If you help them by being a good customer, they will be more likely to help you. It is in their best interests to raise your limit, because that is just more money that you could spend with them. But if you look like you are risky at all, such as by making late payments, they won't want to take the risk.

– Build your case – Have your case ready, with all of the positives that you can think of for why they should give you an increase. Good reasons include any increase in income you have had, a long history of paying your bill on time, the length of time that you have had the card, a low overall credit utilization, and possibly the lack of other debt in your life (if you have just finished paying anything off). If they provide any pushback, you have to be able to clearly state why they are making a wrong decision.

Chapter 14: So Who Looks At Your Credit Report?

Credit reporting agencies, also known as credit bureaus, collect, store and sell information on credit users, in the form of credit reports. They make a profit by providing creditors and lending institutions with information concerning the financial profile and credit history of an individual, such as you. Businesses pay fees to these credit reporting agencies, in return for access to these files.

Credit bureaus get information from your creditors, such as auto finance company, bank, credit union, credit card company, department store, and other credit granting institutions. They also obtain information about you from public records, such as property or court records. Each credit reporting agency obtains its information from different sources, so the information in one credit reporting agency's report may not be the same as the information in another credit reporting agency's report.

Credit reporting agencies do not make decisions regarding your creditworthiness. The credit reporting agencies compile your credit history into a report and pass that along to the potential credit grantor.

Lenders purchase and review your credit report anytime you apply for a loan or credit card. When you apply to buy a cell phone or rent an apartment, someone will probably look at your credit report. And you may be surprised to learn that employers often review your credit report during the hiring process. So having a good credit history can smooth the way in many areas of your financial life.

The Three Major Credit Bureaus

There are three major credit bureaus around the country: Experian, Equifax, TransUnion. The odds are you will have a brush with at least one of these agencies every time you apply for credit with a credit granting institution. Their names and addresses are as follow:

Experian

P.O. Box 2002

Allen, TX 75013

(888) 397-3742

www.experian.com

Equifax

P.O. Box 740241

Atlanta, GA 30374

(800) 685-1111

www.equifax.com

TransUnion

P.O. Box 1000

Chester, PA 19022

(800) 916-8800

www.transunion.com

Obtaining Your Credit Report

First, you need to see what information is contained in your credit report. Nothing can be done to repair your credit until you know what your report says about you.

When you apply for credit — such as a credit card or student loan — the company from which you're seeking credit checks your credit report from one or more of the three major consumer reporting agencies, TransUnion, Equifax, and Experian. In addition to your credit report, they will generally use a credit score like FICO Scores in their evaluation of risk before lending to you.

By law, you can get a free copy of your credit report every year through AnnualCreditReport.com. You can order your report from all three major consumer reporting agencies - Equifax, Experian, and TransUnion - at one time or spread them out throughout the year.

You can also order your free credit report:

By phone: Call (877) 322-8228

By mail: Download and complete the Annual Credit Report Request Form and mail it to the following address:

Annual Credit Report Request

Post Office Box 105281

Atlanta, GA 30348-5281

No matter which method you choose, you have the option to request credit reports from the three major credit reporting agencies all at once or one report at a time.

There are certain times when you are entitled to an additional free copy for special circumstances. The rule that gives you free access once a year does not affect your ability to get a free report in the situations listed below. You are entitled to a free credit report:

If you have been denied credit within the past 60 days

If you are on public welfare assistance

If you are unemployed and intend to apply for employment in the next 60 days

If an adverse decision related to your employment has been made based in whole or in part on information contained in the report

If you have reason to believe your file contains inaccurate information due to fraud or identity theft

If your report has been revised based upon an investigation you request

Paying for Additional Credit Reports

If you have already gotten your free yearly credit report, you can get another for a small fee. To order additional credit reports after you have gotten your free annual report from the Annual Credit Report Service, you must contact the credit bureau (reporting agency) directly. You can do so:

Online. The credit bureaus encourage people to order reports from their websites.

By mail. If you choose to order your report by mail, write them at their address.

By phone. You can call their toll free number.

You will have to provide some personal information so the credit bureau can identify you.

Why Order All Three Credit Reports?

Ordering all three credit reports will give you a complete view of your credit history and let you repair your credit at all three credit bureaus instead of just one. Each credit bureau collects and records information in different ways and may not have the same information about your credit history.

Some of your creditors and lenders might report only to one of the credit bureaus. And, since credit bureaus don't typically share information, it's possible to have different information on each of your reports.

Reviewing Your Report

When you receive your report, examine it carefully. Go through it line by line. Make a list of any errors and negative items that you find. Sometimes there are mistakes on your report that can be hurting you. Don't assume that because it is on your report that it is automatically true.

Damaging information may appear in your report without your knowledge. Make sure all information is current and accurate. Identify any incorrect or inaccurate information that has been entered into your report. Pay close attention to all the accounts listed on your report.

Removing Derogatory or Negative Information From Your Report

There is a method to remove negative or unverifiable information from your credit report. The following technique is based on rights granted to consumers through the Fair Credit Reporting Act. This techniques produces results fast - in as little as one week.

You have the right to dispute any information that is contained in your credit report. If an account is not being reported 100% accurately, by law the credit bureau must remove it from your report. For instance, if a collection agency is reporting a collection on your report and they cannot verify the information, the credit bureau must delete the entry.

Removing negative items from your credit report can also have a huge positive impact on your credit scores.

Section 609 of the Fair Credit Reporting Act

According to the FCRA, if a credit file is on a consumer's bureau it has to be properly verified. Each item included in a credit bureau has a verification piece - but, the bureaus never have it.

It is impossible for the credit bureaus to physically verify millions of credit applications that's hitting them daily because they don't have the man power for that kind of task.

Each month your bank or creditor sends an electronic file with the details of your account to the credit reporting agencies. Then the credit reporting agencies simply put that on your report with NO VERIFICATION as to whether the account is valid, the information is correct or whether the creditor even has the right to report it! But that is not what the law says must be done.

You, the consumer, have a right to receive a copy of the original creditor's documentation. You're not requesting that they go out and get the verifiable proof from the creditor. You are requesting that they provide you with the verifiable proof that they are supposed to have on file already. The credit bureaus do not have them on file.

Since they cannot provide verification to you in the form of a physical contract document per your written request to do so – the account is classified as UNVERIFIED and under the Fair Credit Reporting Act - ALL UNVERIFIED ACCOUNTS MUST BE DELETED.

There is not one single negative item which cannot legally be removed from a credit report if the credit bureaus cannot, or will not provide verifiable proof that the item reported belongs to you.

This credit repair method has proven time and time again to be successful in the removal of questionable negative and derogatory items. It doesn't matter whether your negative items are valid or not.

How To Dispute Negative Information On Your Credit Report

Disputing negative entries on your credit report is the most effective method to delete unfavorable information and improve your credit score.

After the credit reporting agency receives your dispute letter, it must prove that the information is correct, or accept your explanation. If the derogatory information is found to be incorrect or can no longer be verified, it must be deleted from your credit record.

Chapter 15: Dealing With The Debt, I

Really Owe!!!

In this chapter, I will break down how everyone gets paid throughout the process so that you don't feel sorry for the collection company because of the great settlement offers you will make. After you understand how they put up pennies to pay for your debts in order to pocket huge profits, your pity will evolve into a payoff party.

Once you have followed the process of sending out validation letters and holding the companies accountable to the credit laws and your rights, there are two final outcomes:

Outcome #1 – Deletion & Removal

Outcome #2 – Negotiation/Settlement Payoff

Take into account that even if you enter in ligation, an attorney will eventually get you to one of the two results listed above.

The first outcome is usually brought about by the Creditors or Collection Companies not complying with the credit laws and regulations that result in deletion/removal.

The second result occurs when the Creditors or Collection Companies have validated your debt account that forces you to now acknowledge and accept that the debt is genuinely yours. This statement means that it is now time to pay up. The great news is that even though you will have to pay, it doesn't mean that you will have to pay full price for the debt!!!

As soon as you find out that validation has occurred on your debt, the very next thought should be negotiation. In credit terminology, any time you negotiate an amount less than the full amount owed, it is deemed as a settlement. All Collection Companies are in it for the money. Never think for one second that they are not squeezing out as big of a profit possible from you in order to stay in business.

In order for you to understand why you should have 100% confidence when dealing with the collection companies, you should first comprehend their compensation.

It is not until you grasp the profit margins and the process of the Collection Companies, that you will become so self-confident that you might want to start calling them right after you finish reading this section.

How do collection companies and creditor s get paid?

First let me define the difference between the Original Creditor and Collection Companies:

*The Original Creditor – refers to the initial company or individual in which the agreement was originally established.

*A Collection Company – applies to the enterprise in which the original debt was transferred to from the Original Creditor.

Please note: Collection Companies can transfer your debt account to other Collection Companies as well.

As you can see, the Creditor is the person or company that you initially established the agreement and relationship. On the other hand, the Collection Company is the 3rd party in which the Original Creditor transfers your account(s) to. These concepts are vital to the understanding of the entire process because every step in the process can be and must be held accountable. In addition, there are profit margins that flow parallel to this process that I will be pointing out.

The first question you want to ask yourself is, "Why would a Creditor, the original person or company that you established the agreement with, transfer your account to a 3rd party Collection Company?

The reason they would transfer your debt is because of a term called "outsourcing."

The Webster Dictionary defines Outsourcing as:

To send away (some of a company's work) to be done by people outside the enterprise.

Companies have gravitated to outsourcing because when they do they can hand over a transaction or item to a business that specializes specifically in that area. This statement means that now that company can refocus their time and resources back on their company's foundational mission.

For example, a hospital's primary purpose and goal are to treat patients and help as many people as possible with their health care needs. What they are not in the business of doing is running down and taking everyone to court who did not pay their medical bills. As an alternative, they transfer your medical debt account to a Collection Company that will love to call you, harass you, and take over the tedious trial while doing it all in one streamlined process.

Most, if not all, hospitals have an accounting department or a department where they attempt to collect the payments owed by their patients. However, after a certain amount time elapses they send it to the specialists, the Collection Companies.

Businesses usually start reaching out for help from a Collection Company anywhere on average from three to six months from time of delinquency.

In order to fully understand the profits that are generated from the process, let's begin with the two ways that the Original Creditor can get compensated:

Compensation Method #1 – A Collection Company can pay the Original Creditor for their delinquent debt.

Compensation Method #2 – The option to issue the client a 1099-C tax form that allows the Original Creditor to get additional tax benefits as it pertains to your delinquent debt.

To elaborate even more on the first form of compensation, I want to simplify the transfer of debt from the Original Creditor to the Collection agency into two sub-categories, Assigned Debt & Purchased Debt.

Compensation Method #1a (Assigned Debt) – The original Creditor still has ownership of the debt, however, assigns the debt to a Collection Company with the hopes of recouping anywhere from 40% to 75%. Keep in mind, they have already accounted for the Collection Company's fees for "Pursuing" the debt. In addition, the Original Creditor holds the authorization to sue a client or not while at the same time sets the minimum percentage amount of which a Collection Company can accept payment. For example, if you owe $1,000, the Original Creditor can set the standard to accept nothing less than $400.

Compensation Method #1b (Purchased Debt) – The Original Creditor can sell the debt entirely to a Collection Company. Keep in mind that the debts are usually so old, Collection Companies pay pennies on the dollar for the debt. This method of compensation means that the Original Creditor is receiving payment from someone outside of you!!!

The second method the Original Creditor gets compensation is by issuing out 1099-C Tax Forms to clients that have settled their debts for less than the original amount owed. In my research, I have found, some estimate that any settlement for more than $600.00 in savings will trigger a 1099-C Tax Form. For example, if you owed $1,000, but you only paid $300.00, saving over $600.00, it may result in a 1099-C Tax Form being issued to you in the mail.

Please note: This doesn't mean that you are 100% guaranteed to get one issued to you, but is up to the company.

The Original Creditor issues out the 1099-C Tax Form which forces the client to count the settlement savings as additional income. In turn, this benefits the Original Creditor by allowing them to take that same amount as a tax deduction against their company's total revenue.

*Please Note: Please consult your tax accountant or whoever prepares your taxes for more information on the 1099-C Tax Form. Since the tax laws are forever changing, getting their professional advice and discovering all the options available to you will be to your advantage.

These above statements implies that not only can the Original Creditor get compensated from Collection Companies, but they also can get tax breaks from the IRS. Understanding this collection process allows you to make confident decisions as it relates to negotiating and settling your debts.

From the Collection Company's perspective, purchasing old debts outright has become a very lucrative business. They acquire the old debts dirt cheap primarily because so much time has elapsed from the original date of delinquency, which is an indicator that it is less likely going to recoup the amount owed, losing its value. In turn, this is how Collection Company's profits become so enormous.

When you review your credit report the amount that it reports is the amount that Collection Companies, hope you pay. Over the years, I have seen clients pay full price for debts even after it has been in collections for years with no attempt to settle or even negotiate a lower amount. Collection Companies wish more people just pay out with no questions asked, because when people pay "full price" they make "FULL PROFIT."

Think about it, if you originally owed $1,000 and the Collection Company purchased the debt for $100.00. Then if you paid $1,000 with no attempt to negotiate, then the Collection Company just profited $900.00 ($1,000 minus $100.00). A Collection Company's profit margins can be astronomical.

Astonishingly enough, even when the Collection Company settles for half the price they are still making a tremendous amount of profit off you. Let's examine this math more carefully. If the Collection Company drops the settlement to 50% from the example referenced above, they are still making a profit of $400.00 ($500.00 minus $100.00).

If you were making that type of profit from just one account, wouldn't you start your own Collection Company?

This epidemic is the reason there are so many Collection Companies and why they keep popping up left and right, because of the profit margins. In order to bring this process to life, I will utilize a common real-life example to illustrate the timeline of a hospital bill gone wrong.

To start, you go to the hospital and get treated. A few months later you get a bill for $1,000 of which your insurance does not cover. The bill is so high, you end up not being able to pay it. The hospital's in-house accounting department tries to collect the debt from you to no avail. In order to be efficient with their time and resources, they turn your debt over to a Collection Company. The Collection Company is thinking "Profit" in which they pursue you for the highest amount possible praying that you pay the full amount. Since the person ends up utilizing the Settlement/Negotiation Chart in chapter five of this book, they were able to settle their collection debt for only 35% or $350.00. However as an additional tax deduction, or also seen as another monetary benefit for them, the Collection Company sends you out a 1099-C Tax Form at the end of the year. This form gives evidence that your settlement savings should be counted negatively against you as additional income while they count it as a positive deduction in regards to their company.

I am not stating what is right or wrong, but my purpose is for you to not feel sorry for any Collection Company after striking a great settlement agreement. Everyone in the process is getting some advantage with the Collection Companies, of course, at the top!!!

Please note, as I stated previously, have your tax accountant or the person preparing your taxes to confirm the advantages you gain by saving hundreds of dollars on a collection. In general, the settlement savings should far outweigh the 1099-C tax implications overall...

Tactfully speaking, when you are gearing up to make the settlement call to the Collection Company one may ask, "Should I take the first offer?" Through my experience, the answer will be – more than likely, no. The reason you should not accept the first offer is because of what you have learned in the above profit process. As you can recall, everyone in the process is getting some benefit, with the Collection Companies lucratively laughing at the top!!!

So rest assured, the first offer will more than likely not be in your best interest. The Collection Company wants to make the biggest profit off you. Just think about it, the Collection Company focus is not making friends, but is focused on making funds!!!

Additionally, before you call to negotiate and try to settle, you always want to have the money ready and available. The logic behind this is, if in some very rare case in which the Collection Company gives you a surprisingly great offer, it would be in your advantage to jump on it immediately while you are still on the phone with the Collection Company.

The downside of not having the money available, is that some settlement offers are only good just for that day or that specific phone call. You never want to let a great opportunity pass you by because you were not prepared and didn't have everything in place. The first offer is a great gauge to show the mindset and flexibility of the Collection Company.

The "Negotiation/Settlement Chart" in the next chapter shows the average amounts you should expect to pay, in percentages, depending on how long the collection debt has been outstanding or unpaid. For example, your settlement power will increase as the time elapses from the original date of delinquency. When collection companies see that you have not paid the collection in 5 years then the possibility of collecting that debt becomes slim to none.

On the other side of that spectrum, if the collection debt is only six months old then the Collection Company may feel that they have a stronger chance of collecting a higher portion of the debt.

The person you will be talking to at the Collection Company is someone who is being paid to collect the debt. The pay structure of most debt collectors is salary plus commission which means that the more they collect from the client, the more compensation they receive. With that in mind, everyone is trying to make a profit on your transaction and "profits eliminate all emotions."

The most valuable person that you can talk to is the person who takes your call. They are the most important person because they are responsible for either working with you or working against you. They're the one that is standing between you and a paid off debt. You want to be strategic in your communication and to remember "Silence is Golden."

In spite of them stating, "This phone call MAY be recorded" it really means that this one call may not end up actually being recorded. However, one way companies capture conversations and results from each phone call is through notes.

The Collection Company's representative determines the tone of the notes which can either directly or indirectly impact the outcome of the negotiation process. For this cause, I recommend you taking your own notes. Your notes should have the answers to the following questions:

Question #1: What is the representative's name?

Question #2: What is the representative's ID number, if applicable?

Question #3: Do they have a direct extension, just in case the call drops?

Question #4: Can the representative confirm the account number of the debt in the system?

Question #5: What time did the call start and when did the call end?

Question #6: What position does the person hold in the company, in which you are speaking to?

Question #7: What information do they have on their system as it pertains to your file? (This question is crucial because you don't what to give out more information than necessary, always letting them speak first...)

These above issues are not only essential for notation purposes but also vital if the Collection Company attempts to use any abusive, deceptive or unfair collection practices during the call. In that case, you will be well equipped having all the information needed in order to file a complaint.

The final question that I am about to touch on is probably the shortest question of them all, but the one that will get you the farthest – which is...

The Most Important Question: **How is your day going?**

This one question is usually missed, but can make the biggest impact. In spite of them being paid a commission and seeing you as just another number, this one question helps everyone to refocus and realize that both parties are still human.

Majority of the time, most people will just say fine or O.K., but there will be some that will open up and become transparent. Those are the ones that will say something like, "Thanks for asking." Now, if they reply that this is the worst day of their life, and they are mad at the world, watch out!!! This question at least gives an opportunity to see if you want to talk to this person or call back and try for another representative!

Think of it as if you were going to the doctor's office and the nurse walks in with a needle and their face is red and full of frustration. Wouldn't you want them to wait a minute and relax and calm down before just start sticking you???

The Most Powerful Question: Is the settlement offer too high or is it low enough for me to benefit from?

Overall, the most dynamic aspect of asking questions are the results or answers that are captured by taking detailed notes as you listen attentively. The detailed notes will help you make more informed decisions and will allow you to access if the settlement offer is too high or is it low enough for you to ultimately benefit.

Consequently, in the process of negotiations you will eventually have to deal with the "most commonly avoided" nine letter word: **rejection**. It is a fact of life that no one likes to get rejected. No matter what the situation is, rejection is viewed upon negatively. However, in this process, it is the tool that helps you discover the limits and the flexibility of the Collection Companies. So even though you might have to experience rejection, remember that the greatest outcome may result in you striking one of the best deals in your life!!!

Points to remember:

*Collection Companies profit way more than they have paid.Collection Companies wish more people pay "FULL PRICE" so they can make a "FULL PROFIT."

*Negotiations involve the risk of being rejected; however, it may also lead to the great reward, - striking one of the best deals in your life!!!

*Face the fact that you now actually owe the debt, and it is your responsibility to fix it. As the saying goes, "You are the best person for the job!!!"

In the next chapter, we will explore what is perhaps the root cause of your pain and more than likely the source behind why you are emotionally drained...

Chapter 16: Keep Your Credit Score Safe

If you have a lower credit score that you would like, odds are that the score is caused by some small financial mistake or oversight you have made in the past. Not every person with bad credit has a low credit score caused by something they did, though. Sometimes, other people's criminal activity can affect your credit score. There are a few tips that can keep you and your credit safe form online and financial predators:

Tip #8: Look out for identity theft. Many people who are careful about paying bills on time and having minimal debts are shocked each year to find that they have low credit scores. In many cases, this happens as a result of identity theft. Identity theft is a type of crime in which people take your personal information and steal that information to pose as you in order to get access to your accounts or identity.

For example, someone with your PIN numbers can remove small amounts of money from your bank account each month or someone can use your name and personal information to get credit cards in your name and use those credit cards with no intention of paying back the money. You are stuck with the large debts and the poor credit score.

To prevent identity theft, always check your account statements carefully each month. Report any suspicious activity or any charges you don't recognize at once. Also check your credit report regularly and immediately investigate any new credit accounts you do not recognize - this is the best way of detecting and acting on identity theft.

If you have been the victim of identity theft, report to the police at once and get a police statement. Send copies of this to your bank and credit bureaus. Better yet, get the credit bureaus to attach the report to your credit report, if you can. Close all your accounts and reopen new ones. You should not have to pay for someone else's illegal activity.

Tip #9: Practice safe banking, safe computing, and safe business practices. To stay safe from identity theft, always follow safe banking and financial practices:

1) Keep account numbers and PIN numbers safe. Cover your account and PIN numbers when using debit at the store and refuse to give your PIN number to anyone. Avoid writing down your PIN and account numbers - you never know when this information could fall into the wrong hands.

2) Only do business with businesses you trust.

3) If you get applications for credit cards in the mail that are "pre-approved" rip up the applications and enclosed letters before discarding them. No, this is not paranoid. Identity thieves sometimes go through garbage in order to find these forms so that they can fill them out and steal your identity.

4) If you use a computer, install good firewall and antivirus protection system and update it religiously. Better yet, take a course in safe computing at your local college or community center. You will learn many good tips for keeping all your information safe while you are online.

5) Never buy anything online from a company you do not trust of from a company that does not have encryption technology and a good privacy policy.

6) Even with all computer precautions, avoid providing private information through email or your computer. Be especially cautious if you get an email from your bank asking you to verify your information by clicking on a link - this is a popular scam that comes not from your bank but from criminals posing as your bank. Ignore the email and phone your bank about the message.

7) Be wary of unsolicited emails, phone calls, or mail advertisements. Most are from legitimate companies but there are companies who promise you a credit card

over the telephone only to charge your existing credit card without sending you anything.

Similarly, letters will sometimes promise you specific items or services. Once you send in your credit card information (usually to a post office box) you hear no more from the company. If you need or want to buy something from a company, be sure to check the company's standing with the Better Business Bureau first.

Send a money order instead of a check (which had your account number) or your credit card information. If you do use a credit card, report any unusual charges or any payments you made for a product that did not arrive to the credit card company.

In some cases, they can stop payment or refund your money as well as take steps to keep your credit card number safe.

8) Be wary of offers that seem too good to be true. If you get an offer for a ten million dollar check - for which you need to put down $5000 as a "sign if good faith"...if you get an offer for a free state-

of-the art computer - if only you provide your account information... take a deep breath and consider before sending in your money and your information.

Offers that are too good to be true always are. Scam artists often rely on your belief in others and your trust to make money. They depend on the fact that you will be so excited about a product or service that you will throw good judgment out the window. Prove them wrong.

When faced with an offer that seems too good to be true, do some research on the web, through the Better Business Bureau, or ask the person making the offer some questions. Never take someone up on an offer that you have been given unsolicited unless the company and the offer both check out.

9) Read the fine print. Some services or companies will have tiny print in their contract or agreement that allows them to charge you extra hidden fees or that allows them to retract certain offers. If

you get an offer through email or the mail, make it a habit to read the fine print.

10) Be alert for a sudden disruption in your mail service. If you do not get mail for some time, contact your post office and ask whether your address was recently submitted for a "change of address" service. It sounds strange, but it's true.

One way that criminals steal identities is to change your address at the local post office. They redirect your mail to a post office box number and steal your mail looking for personal information such as bank statements, pre-approved credit card applications, and other pieces of mail they can use to steal your identity.

They use this information to pose as you with lenders and run up huge charges in your name. Simply keeping an eye out on your mail can help you keep your credit score safe.

Tip #10: Check your credit score regularly
You are more likely to notice problems and inconsistencies if you check your credit score on a regular basis - at least

once a year and preferably three times a year. Be sure to check your credit rating with each credit bureau, too. If you notice anything odd or anything you don't recognize (such as a charge account you did not open) report it immediately.

Sometimes, these errors are caused by mistakes made at the credit bureau, but they could be an indication that someone is using your identity. In either case, such mistakes could hurt your credit score. Fixing such errors improves your credit score. If you think you have been the victim of identity theft, take action at once:

1) Contact the three major credit bureaus and ask to speak to the fraud department. Explain that you have been the victim of identity theft (or believe you may have been) and ask that an "alert" be placed on your file. This will let anyone looking at your report know that you may have been the victim of fraud. It will also mean that you will be alerted any time a lender asks to look at your file - each time a lender

does look at your file, it may be an indication that the identity thieves are trying to open a new account in your name.

When the lender sees that the person applying is not you, they will deny the thieves credit and in most cases the criminals will stop trying to access your identity. Most alerts on your file last 90 or 180 days but you can extend this period to several years by asking the credit agencies for an extension of the "fraud alert" in writing.

In some states, you can even ask for a freeze to be placed on your credit score and credit report which will prevent anyone but yourself and those creditors you already have from accessing your file. Any lenders the thieves contact to set up a new account will be refused access and the thieves will not be able to get any more money in your name.

You are entitled to a free copy of your credit report if you have been the victim of identity theft. Be sure to take advantage of this offer so that you can check exactly how your credit has been affected. Dispute those items that are not yours.

2) Call the Federal Trade Commission (FTC) at 1-877-438-4338. This is the special hotline that the FTC has set up to help customers deal with fraud and identity theft. You will be able to get up-to-date information about your rights and advice as to what you can do to improve your credit score and keep in safe in the future.

3) Contact the police. Identity theft is a crime and you need to file a police report (be sure to keep a copy of this report) so that you can help the police potentially catch the criminals responsible. Contacting the police will also give you a paper trail and proof that a crime has been committed. Keeping a paper trail of the crime and your response will make it easier for you to repair your credit if it has been damaged by identity thieves.

4) Contact your creditors or any creditors that the identity thieves have opened an account with. Ask to speak to the security

department and explain your predicament. You may need to have your accounts closed or at least your passwords changed to protect yourself.

You may also need to fill out a fraud affidavit to state that a crime has been committed - be sure to keep a copy of this form for your records. The security team of the creditors should be able to advise you as to what you can do. Be sure to note down who you contacted and when so that you have records of the steps you have taken to deal with the crime.

If you have been the victim of identity theft and you are deeply in debt to creditors you never contacted, you will not be held responsible for the charges - but you will have to prove that you have been the victim of identity theft, which is tricky since the thieves are using your name and claiming to be you.

It is a frustrating experience because lenders will want to be paid and you will want to avoid paying for charges you did not run up. Being persistent and keeping good proof that you have been the victim of a crime will help to clear your credit score. In the meantime, however, you will be faced with a much lower credit rating than you deserve and you may have to put off larger purchases that may require a loan.

Chapter 17: Create A Budget

We all know we should create a budget, but many of us either just don't want to make one or don't know where to start.

A budget is the best way to plan for and keep track of your monthly income and expenses. It will help to determine how much is coming in, how much is going out and how much is left over. It will also help to determine if what's left should be saved or can be spent on wants rather than needs. Budgets also come in handy when it comes to debt management.

In order to gain control over debt, it is important to set up a budget and maintain it. This is the tricky part. It takes a certain level of commitment on the part of the individual to stick to the budget. Otherwise, it just becomes a plan that is never implemented.

That is where most people fail. They do manage to set up a budget, but after a few weeks, for whatever reason, they stray from what the plan.

How to Set Up a Budget

Budgeting doesn't have to be painful or difficult. One of the reasons people avoid budgeting like the plague is because it means making tough decisions about "cutting back" or "making sacrifices".

Here are a few actionable steps to take in order to create a budget:

Step 1: Know how much you have.

If you have savings, or investments, check your account balances and write them down. Checking account balances too, write them down.

Step 2: Know where your money comes from.

Identify all your sources of incomes i.e. job, child support, disability or unemployment, etc.

To make your budget more realistic, only use fixed earnings, or those that you are sure to receive. Uncertain income such as tips, a potential raise, or a commission-based bonus should be excluded.

Step 3: Know where your money goes.

Identify your expenses. It helps to use categories.

·Fixed expenses like rent or mortgage, car payment, childcare, insurance, etc.

·Basic necessities, i.e. groceries, clothing, gas, etc.

·Discretionary expenses i.e. gifts, dining out, entertainment, etc.

To figure out how much you spend, save all your receipts for a 30-day period and refer to them when calculating average monthly expenses. It also helps to go over previous month's bank statements and check your transaction history. Get receipts from gas station purchases, especially if you use cash.

There are also several different tools and software products that you can use to keep track of your actual income and expenses. There are several free apps and online tools to help develop a budget if you are not comfortable doing it the old-school way of using pen and paper.

Step 3: Know how much you owe.

You should already have an idea how much you are paying for your various debts every month. However, you should also find out the total amount of debt you currently have, and this encompasses your various loans, mortgages, and even credit cards.

Step 4: Compare your income and expenses.

By examining your income versus your expenses, you will immediately know whether you are overspending, spending just right, or spending so little you have extra money each month. This will then guide you on where your budgeting will go next.

If your expenses exceed your income you need to examine where you need to reduce spending.

·Make cuts. When you logged your expenses, you categorized them according to the nature of the expense. You may also use the log to refine the list further, classifying them according to necessity. Identify the expenses that are not necessary and cut them out.

·Make adjustments. Some experts recommend categorizing expenses in two ways: needs and wants (and the identification should be done objectively). When making a trip to the grocery store, list the items you need and set a spending limit for only those items. Purchase items on the want list only if there is enough money left after all other expenses are taken care of.

·Look for alternatives to spending. For example, instead of going to the movies four times in a month, you may want to cut it down to only twice a month. Ask yourself: Do I really need to pay to watch the IMAX version when the regular theater is $3.00 less? And why buy movie theater candy when the local discount store has the same thing for $0.99?

Step 5: Treat "Savings" as a regular expense.

Decide on an amount to regularly put into your savings account, or any other savings vehicle, such as stock investments and financial instruments. If you can set aside 10% of your take-home pay every month and do this on a recurring basis, as you would an expense, you'll increase your savings faster. If your job offers direct deposit, you can have a portion of your check deposited into savings every pay period. That way you don't have to think about it.

Step 6: Test your budget.

Don't expect the first few weeks of putting your budget into action to be easy. There will be a transition period as you change your spending habits. sHowever, do not make that an excuse not to follow the budget diligently.

Keep detailed records of your daily spending for at least a month; this will help you assess whether your budget is working, and if you are truly adhering to the plan.

You should also use the testing period as an opportunity to make necessary adjustments. It is possible that you overlooked some expenses or other factors while you were drafting your budget.

Tips for an Effective Budget

A budget is never set in stone. There will be constant adjustments as circumstances change. Priorities change, and unavoidable situations demand that changes be made.

In order to ensure the budget remains effective, however, here are some simple tips that could help.

Ø Keep it simple. Many people don't stick with their budget because they're too overwhelmed by the smallest details. Keep things simple if detail orientation isn't your strong suit. If you personally prepared the budget, however, this shouldn't be a problem.

Ø Keep it realistic. Budgeting makes use of estimates, but these estimates are based on actual, historical figures. Don't pull amounts or numbers out of thin air or without basis. Otherwise, you're just setting your budget – and yourself – up for failure.

Ø Value substance over form. So what if your recordkeeping is less than systematic? It doesn't matter if your budget is written in a small notebook instead or a spreadsheet. As long as you understand what you've written, and it contains all the necessary information, you are doing great.

Ø Stick to it. The most difficult part of a budget is sticking to it. Just remind yourself why you're doing this and what the end result will be.

Chapter 18: Cut The Credit Cards

If you're looking to save some money then you need to make sure you're spending less. That means getting rid of all those credit cards. If you have a lot of credit cards you're going to be tempted to use them and that's not going to help you save anything. So what you want to do is get rid of the credit cards.

One thing it's important to remember is that actually closing out your credit cards is probably going to decrease your credit score. When you have less available credit (the amount of money that the credit card companies allow you to spend) your amount of credit used increases. What you want to do is make sure that you keep a few credit cards so you have a decent amount of available credit. You want to avoid using them however.

If you're able to avoid the temptation to purchase things you can put one credit card in the back of your purse or wallet.

Choose a card that will work anywhere such as a major credit card company. This is for emergencies only. An emergency doesn't mean you found something that you really want to have. It means that your car broke down and needs to be towed, or you run out of gas.

The rest of the credit cards you decide to keep should be locked up somewhere in your home. Put them in a safe or lockbox. This way you have to actively think about getting the card out again before you're able to actually use it. This will keep you from using the card in a spur of the moment fashion and will ensure that you still have it available if absolutely necessary.

Stop using credit cards as much as possible. This will allow you to save more money because you won't have to spend a lot of your money on credit card bills at the end of the month. Instead, you'll have all the money you would have spent on those bills left over to put in a savings account. Remember that budget you made at the beginning of this book and make sure that you stick to it. Don't spend too much of your money on things you don't need throughout the month.

Keep in mind that if you don't use your credit card at all it's eventually going to be taken away from you. That's because the credit card companies don't want to allow credit to someone that isn't going to do anything with it and eventually they will cancel your account. This is going to lower the amount of available credit you have and it's going to decrease your credit score.

The best thing to do is make one to two small purchases on your credit card every few months. Try to space out using different cards so that none of them get taken but you don't owe very much money each month. You want to keep the amount negligible. That means it's low enough that it really doesn't affect your overall budget. This is going to let you keep the card but, at the same time, it's not going to completely break the bank.

Chapter 19: Ask For A Credit Line Increase

More often than not, people assume that increasing your credit card limit undeniably lower their credit score. In fact, some people just ask for a higher credit limit when they have charged up to their maximum, while others contact the company for an increase without even giving it a second thought.

Why Should You Ask For A Credit Line Increase?

Interestingly, increasing your credit line can actually boost your credit score to a great extent. If you have low credit utilization percentage, increasing your credit line will drastically increase your credit score.

In other words, if you use lesser of your available credit, your credit score will improve. In fact, financial experts recommend that you do not use more than half of your limit on your credit cards. By asking your creditors to increase your

149

credit limit on your existing card, you are minimizing your credit card utilization percentage.

Increasing Your Credit Line Vs Getting A New Card

Yup. That's a tough one. The biggest benefit of requesting a credit line increase over applying for a new credit card is that your credit record will not show up any inquiry. When you apply for a new credit card, creditors are bound to do a credit check on your credit report Any searches done on your credit report will be treated as a normal credit inquiry by credit reporting agencies, and this may be a negative impact on your credit score.

Step-By-Step Instruction On How To Request For A Credit Line Increase:

☐Last Six Months Consistent Payment– predictably, you will be expected to pay your credit card bills on time, so the first thing to make sure is that you have been consistently paying your bills for the last six months.

☐Credit Utilization Ratio - your credit utilization is pretty much how credit bureaus estimate your credit score. For instance, if your total credit limit is $5000 and you have used $4900 your credit utilization ratio is EXTREMELY HIGH. On the other hand, if you have only used as little as $300 on the card that gives you $5000 limit, your utilization ratio is EXTREMELY LOW. You want to keep your utilization ratio extremely low. Hence, if you have multiple cards, try considering credit card balance transfer.

☐Figure Out The Right Card - you need to figure out which card you want your credit increase on. DO NOT go to every credit card company and ask for limit increase because this would lead to multiple credit checks on your credit report that can hurt your credit score and pull it down by 10 points. So, it's extremely important that you decide which card you want to go forward with.

☐Supporting Documents- sometimes it might be necessary to produce documents that prove your credit worthiness. So make sure you have enough supporting documents with you like:

1.Income

2.Any occupation change

3.Debt record

4.your relationship with the credit agency

□Contact your creditor- you can put in your request with an online auction or go directly to the credit card agency. You can also do this over a phone call and ask them to increase your credit card limit.

Just because you have more credit at your mercy, doesn't mean that you have to go crazy with it. The less money you spend on your card, the better it is to boost your credit score.

Chapter 20: Alternatives To Student Loans

The best way to stay out of student loan debts is find alternative way to paid for an education. Financial aid, grants, scholarships, two year colleges and trade school are options to help you reach your educational goals and secure a career. We will discuss these avenues in this chapter.

Financial aid is an excellent source of college funding, aid includes grants, scholarships, work-study and federal student loans to help you pay for college. It's a common misconception that financial aid is available only to low-income families. This is a false idea because many states offer grants to students based on merit rather than need. Some offer low rates and deferred repayment financial aid options to almost all students seeking financial aid for college and education. Here is a list of the most common federal grants:

Pell Grants are federal grants designated to students with financial need. These grants are awards if criteria are met. The great part of this funding they don't need to be repaid and your eligibility for them will be determined by the results of your Free Application for Student Aid, or FAFSA which determines the student's eligibility by using, the Expected Family Contribution or (EFC) formula, a standard calculation set by the United States Department of Education. The maximum amount that the government funds for each applicant is $5,645. Students who received a full scholarship of any kind doesn't qualify for this grant.

Federal Supplemental Educational Opportunity Grant (FSEOG) program is a grant for students with the greatest financial need. A student eligible for the grant can receive between $100 and $4,000 depending on the intended college and Expected Family Contribution. This grant it is awarded to schools by the federal government and is a college-based grant for undergraduates.

154

The Teacher Education Assistance for College and Higher Education (TEACH) is a grant that offers financial assistance for educators who will work in low-income, high-need fields of study. The grant program was designed in 2007 through the College Cost Reduction and Access Act and eligible students may receive up to $4,000 per year.

The Iraq and Afghanistan Service Grant (IASG) is grant is for students whose parent or guardian was a member of the U.S. armed forces and died as a result of performing military service in Iraq or Afghanistan after the events of 9/11. This is a non-need-based grant for students ineligible for a Federal Pell Grant due only to having less financial need than is required to receive Pell funds. Students must have been less than 24 years old or enrolled at least part-time at an institution of higher education at the time of the parent's or guardian's death. The current annual award grants up to $5,311.71 for qualifying individuals. For information go to Grants.gov at http://www.grants.gov/.

Scholarships are awarded based upon various criteria and money is not required to be repaid. The granter scholarships usually reflect the values and purposes of the donor or founder of the award and are commonly in these categories:

Merit-based are the most common scholarships, private organizations awarded the scholarships for academic achievement or high scores on standardized tests with other reasons that matches the organizations' vision for the scholarship program. Most scholarships are paid directly by the institution the student attends, rather than issued directly to the student.

Need-based are for students with financial needs for tuition, room, board, books, transportation and school supplies. Some private need-based awards are confusingly called scholarships, and require the results of a FAFSA.

Student-specific are scholarships based upon gender, race, religion, family and medical history, or many other student-specific factors. Minority scholarships are the most common awarded in this student specific category.

Athletic scholarships are sports based scholarships awarded to students with exceptional skill in a sport. The college awards the student the scholarship to play the sport on their college team.

Career-specific these are scholarships are awarded to students who pursue a specific field of study, often times the student will need to work in a high-need community.

College-specific scholarships are often given on the basis of academic and personal achievement. Universities and colleges give these highly qualified individual scholarships to attract them to their institution.

For more information on scholarships U.S. Department of Labor's at http://careerinfonet.org/scholarshipsearc h/ScholarshipCategory.asp?searchtype=ca tegory&nodeid=22

Two-year colleges

Two year colleges are one of the best options to the road to a college degree. Cheaper, quicker, and highly vocational, two-year schools offer students the chance to start their careers sooner and with less no debt with Financial Aid Programs because the average cost of tuition and fees at a two-year school is only $3,131, just over one-third of the cost for a year at a four-year public institution. Two-year students typically either focus on taking general pre-requisite courses that can transfer to a four-year institution or courses in their specific trade. When a two-year college student transfers to a four year college; the student still receives a bachelor's degree with the four year college institution name. Two-year colleges' offers course with flexibility so many classes offered through community or technical colleges can be taken in the evening or on weekends. Students have an option to work a part-time or full-time job while they earn their degree.

Trade School and Vocational School

A trade school, also known as a technical or vocational school, is an educational institution that exists to teach skills related to a specific job. Trade schools are a more streamlined approach to education, with curricula focusing on developing a particular skill set and knowledge base and have smaller class sizes, and the majority of the training is hands-on. The schools typically take less than two years to complete. You can get well paying jobs by going to Vocational schools like electrician, mechanic, machinist, pharmacy technician, medical biller and dental hygienist. Trade school average costs are $33,000, which, compared to a $127,000 bachelor's degree. A student can save $94,000. The biggest factor is job security most of the jobs training you acquire at a trade school are extremely difficult to export to another country. More and more jobs are being outsourced to places where labor is cheaper, making domestic employment in certain sectors where bachelor's degrees are required difficult to get in this economy.

Employer Education Programs

Many employers have incentive programs for higher education or for job training in a trade field. Companies many time have to pay high cost for training for new employees and finding qualified applicants so many employers will promote current employees already within the company in the will get the necessary education for the job position. Employers may also have education programs for employees' family members. You should ask your employer if they have education programs available.

In conclusions, student loans can a benefit to your financial future if you properly plan on your career goals and consider your payment options. You should always look for Financial Aid, grants and scholarship to reduce the cost of your education. When student and parent borrows don't not understate the terms and cost of the repayment of student loans it can lead to financial disaster.

Chapter 21: Fixing Your Credit Scorefast

Having a poor credit score can not only negatively affect you financially - it can lead to lost job opportunities, rejected applications for tenancies and other seriously debilitating problems. If you have a credit score that could use a bit more than a simple boost, then you know exactly how it seems to follow you wherever you go. If you're sick and tired of always being refused for a credit card or paying more in interest rates just because you have poor credit, then it's time to use these fast fixes for your credit score - and get back on track right away:

Stop throwing your money at debts like your mortgage and student loan; instead, start focusing on paying off your credit card bills and any personal loans that you may have, as these kinds of debts drastically affect your credit score more than the other debts. While you may want to own your home faster or get rid of that student loan sooner, it's important to realize that this won't do much for your score. Yet when it comes to that one single credit card balance, you can really skyrocket your score just by throwing your money at it. When it comes to debt, it really pays to have the right ones taken care of first.

Don't spend more on your plastic than what you can pay. Credit reporting agencies frown on people who aren't able to live within their means, which a balance on your credit card indicates. Create a household budget that sticks to your income, and make sure you don't over-exceed what you make by using your credit cards to fund that shopping spree.

Know your limits. It's a simple move that can save you big in the long run. Why is this, you ask? Simple: if you spend over your limit, not only will credit reporting agencies give you a black mark on your report - you'll end up having to pay some pretty hefty fees! This money is better spent paying off the principal of your debt, not some outrageous fees that go straight into a banker's pocket. Additionally, make sure that credit reporting agencies have your limits correct - often your credit score can be lowered unfairly if an agency has the wrong information. Call them on it and get your report updated for an instant boost.

Don't close any old credit card accounts that you might have. Your credit score is determined by the amount of credit versus debt that you have; therefore, the more credit you have (without balances, that is) the higher your credit score will be. This shows credit reporting agencies that you are trustworthy enough for lenders without living beyond your means.

Ask for a goodwill adjustment, where a happy lender might just erase a late payment from your credit score if you've been displaying good credit behavior. Wait for a year after making payments on time to request this, and you'll be seeing an improved score in no time!

Having a poor credit history does not necessarily mean it's the end of your future finance eligibility. Follow this guide and be pro-active in the repair of your credit rating, and you will soon see fruits of your efforts.

The best way on how to improve credit score quickly if you have a bad credit record is to perform self-credit repair! Self-credit repair is a procedure where you argue unfavorable items on your credit report with the three main credit bureaus. This will involve sending argument letters to the three credit agencies to fix your credit score.

When these letters are received by the three credit agencies, they will try to examine your argument with your lender who is reporting about the negative items on your credit report. They will have 30 days to react and if they fail to give supporting evidence within the time given, the negative items will be removed from your credit report.

This is actually a simple process to fix your credit score. If you have ever been turned down for a loan or insurance that you wanted, you know that it does not sound right to you. In most cases, there may be some items that are reporting incorrectly on your credit report and you should start investigating and do a credit repair yourself in a reasonable time frame.

How to Fix Your Credit Yourself

The most important thing you need to do right away is to obtain a complete history of your credit report to understand what has been going on in the past. Look closely to locate each item that could cause a red flag or lower your FICO scores on your credit report.

What am I looking for precisely?

While looking over your credit information you want to first locate any discrepancy. Mistakes on your information are accounts that contain information that is not correct. It might be something regarding behind payment being recorded and you know you were never late for this payment. Another area you may also want to look at to fix your credit score is any over-limit items that are reported incorrectly and the credit bureaus assume that you are consistent in excess of your credit limit.

In addition, check for disparaging information such as delayed payments, charged off accounts, sets, rulings and economic failure. All of these will drag your credit score down quick.

What Steps Should I perform to Correct These Accounts?

This is a crucial step on how to improve credit score. First, create a list of these accounts so they are separated from your fine accounts. Make sure that you position these accounts so that the oldest accounts are listed first and the latest accounts are listed last.

Then, you will need to issue credit argument correspondence letters to the first two accounts for each credit agency that is reporting the unfavorable information on this account. This is essential since there are three agencies and they all report in a different method so you want to make sure that you are not transferring an argument letter to an agency that is not reporting wrongfully about you!

What should go on a Credit Argument Correspondence Letter and Why I am Writing It?

This correspondence is essentially telling the agencies that you do not have the same opinion with the information they are reporting on your credit report. The credit argument letter you are writing should contain your account number, name, address and social security number.

How Will a Correspondence Assist Me to Repair My Credit?

Once your correspondence is received, the credit agencies, under Federal Law, have to examine this information with the original lender. If the original lender does not or will not give evidence of the information, then the agencies will have to eliminate the negative item from your report. Once the negative item on your credit report is detached, your scores will increase and your credit will be repaired a little. In some occasions, your score may jump up 20 to 50 points!

This method of how to raise your credit score may vary depends on each individual situation and the nature of the negative item you originally have. Practicing on different available tools is very often the key to successfully fix your credit score.

Chapter 22: Credit Repair Strategies

Where to Start Repairing Your Credit

If you realize that your score is low, there are certain drastic measures you need to take in order to address the situation.

-Stop using credit cards. If your circumstances demand that you must use a credit card at some point, use the credit cards with the lowest interest rate. Cheap is the catch phrase for you now because you are trying to resolve a credit score crisis. It has a lot to do with your spending habits.

-Deposit as much as you can to the cards that charge the highest interest. Just meet the minimum for the other cards in the meantime. This is one of debt recovery strategies. It is more like an inverted snowball approach.

-Don't open new credit accounts as you are trying to repair your damaged credit score rating. Don't jump from one problem to the next. New credit accounts will simply lead you down the same road of destruction as has happened in the current situation.

-Avoid opening new credit accounts in a short span of time. This often happens when you are looking for funding for college. Although some agencies have a waiver for such enquires if they are done within a span of a month, others still consider such applications and factor them in your credit report. You are therefore advised to spend a much shorter time shopping for funding for your college fees. The exceptions notwithstanding, such acts are generalized considered an indication of poor financial management.

Let's take a look at the strategies you can use to repair your credit.

Pay to delete

In this strategy, you agree to pay a creditor only if they agree to delete such items from the credit report. I mentioned about zero balances; don't fall for the trap of creditors who say they will mark it as zero. Zero is not good for you because it shows you have been having problems in the past (this sticks in your credit report for 7 or more years)! In simple terms, your report shouldn't be showing that you have had a bad credit history with derogatory items. If the creditor is interested in their money more than tainting your credit, they will agree to this. If the information passes to collection agencies after 2 years, you can also use this strategy to make them stop reporting your settled debt; in any case, they buy the debts for a tiny fraction so anything they get will probably be good enough! This is the best time (when the debt is with the collection agencies) to use the pay to delete strategy because you have more bargaining power. If the collection agency doesn't accept your offer, its only option is through a judgment.

Note#1: Use pay to delete when you start noticing new derogative items in your report since these could easily hurt your credit. You might even start seeing multiple collection companies reporting the same debt. In such times, you have an advantage since you negotiate everything on your terms; if one does not accept your offer, another will definitely take it.

Note#2: Have everything put in writing if they agree on your terms. If they cannot put it in writing, don't pay. After paying, you should give it about 45 days to reflect in your credit report. Don't take anything less than deletion; don't accept updating balance. If they cannot delete, don't pay. The process is pretty fast so they shouldn't give you excuses that they cannot delete; mention the Universal Data Form to make them know that you know that it is possible.

Note#3: Choose your battles well i.e. Don't use this strategy on creditors who have a lot to lose because they might sue you to compel you to pay. Aim for creditors who have already been barred by statute of limitation (2 years have passed), which means they cannot sue you in court to compel you to pay.

Identify theft claim

Over 16 million Americans are victims of identity theft. This is definitely a large population so anyone could be a victim. Identity theft is a crime, which involves the police so ensure you are ready to go this route. If you are sure that your score has been ruined because of identity theft, you can use this method. Abusing this method could land you into trouble with the law. Here is how to dispute using the method:

Step 1: Report the matter to the police then get a copy of your report from the local sheriff (you will need this report later)

Step2: File the dispute with FTC using this link here.

Step 3: Go on to dispute with various credit bureaus.

Step4: Set up an identity theft alert (be sure to know what this means in terms of your access to credit).

Lookout for errors in the report

I mentioned that 93% of the credit reports have been proven to have errors. Look out for any of these then file a dispute. Such things like last date of activity, write off date, wrong account name or number and others could be enough to taint your credit. Don't overlook any of that. If the report really has an error, don't be discouraged by the credit bureau's stalling tactics; mention the Notice (Summons) and complaint to make them know that you are really aware of what the law requires of them. The bureaus wouldn't want to have their systems investigated and proven to be weak/flawed so this strategy can actually compel them to correct errors thus boosting your credit.

Pay the original creditor

You don't want multiple collection agencies reporting new items every month since this hurts your score. Simply send a check with full payment of the outstanding amount to the original creditor then send proof of the payment to the collection agencies that have reported that debt. After that, you then request that they should delete all the derogatory items from your credit report. You can blend this with the pay to delete strategy mentioned above.

Request for proof of the original debt

If you are sure that the credit card has been written off due to late payment, there are times when the carriers might not have the original billing statements within 30days as stipulated by the law. With this, you can get the item removed from your report such that it appears as if the entry was not even there. You can also request for the original contract that you actually signed when applying for a credit card. You shouldn't just ask for verification because by doing so, you ask the collection agency to verify that they received your request for collection on an account that bears your name. You should be clear on what you want them to do; in this case, they should provide proof of debt including giving you statements for the last few months and the original contract, which you signed.

Settle your debt

Total debt owed accounts for up to 30% of the credit score so don't overlook this. This includes personal loans, car loan, and credit utilization. You should also calculate the credit utilization ratio (the balance you carry in your revolving fund compared to your credit). As your credit utilization increases, your credit score goes down; aim to keep your credit card balances no more than 30% of your credit card limit. You should even aim for zero balances since this means higher credit score. Combine this strategy with pay to delete strategy.

To pay your debts, you can use the snowballing or avalanching strategies. Snowballing involves paying off debts with the lowest balance first then closing them as you move up to the bigger debts. Avalanching involves paying debts starting from those with the highest interest rates as you move down.

Settle your bills promptly

Payment history accounts for 35% of your credit score making it one of the biggest determinants of the score. This is pretty straight forward; when you pay your bills on time, your score will improve. You could even set up automatic payments just to ensure that you won't miss payments since the amounts are deducted from your account. The biggest contributors to this include collections, bankruptcies, and different late payments. You should not that the recent delinquencies have greater effect than the old ones; 70% of the score is determined by whatever has happened within the past 2 years.

Mix/spread your credit

This usually affects your credit score by up to 10%. Having more types of credit signifies that you can handle your finances properly making you credit worthy especially if you have a good payment history.

Handy tips to improve your score

*Avoid Bad Signals

One of the subtle indications that your report may pick and affect you negatively includes using your credit card to a pawnshop. Although it is not an objective assessment of your financial situation, the readership will develop qualms about you. Such actions speak volumes about your financial organization ability.

*Do Not Delete Your Past Good Debt Records

Your credit history speaks volumes about your consistency. This is the information the lender looks for to decide whether you are a good or bad risk.

*Use fewer cards

The small nuisance balances on your cards adversely affect your score. Many people do not realize that it is more expensive to use more credit cards. It is even harder to manage them. Consequently, the chance of defaulting or making a late payment is significantly increased when you use several cards.

*Minimize the lowest interest rate loan hunt period

When you apply for many loans within a short period, the credit report often reflects several loans instead of the final one you might have settled on a month later.

*Get a settlement letter when you settle any debt then send the letter to the different bureaus to have any derogatory items removed.

Watch out for Fair Debt Collection Practices Act (FDCPA) Violations

The law is on your side when it comes to the manner in which the debt collection agencies can collect debts from you. If they violate these, you can actually compel them to delete your derogatory entries since the penalties they will pay far exceed the amount that might be outstanding (some fines could go as high as $10,000). Actually, every violation has a penalty of $1000 payable to you! Here are some of the things to watch out for.

- If the creditor calls you before 8.00 am in the morning

- If they call after 9.00 pm

- If they call you at your place of work persistently

- If they call third parties. Creditors are only allowed to call your spouse apart from you for purposes of tracing you.

- If they inform someone else and inform them that they are trying to recover debt from you.

- If they call you after you have officially notified them not to call you.

- If they contact you after you have officially informed them that you are being represented by an attorney.

You can effectively defend yourself by reporting to the FDCPA if you are subjected to the following:

*If they try to collect invalid debt. This happens more frequently than most people know. It happens due to various reasons; some are deliberate while others are accidental. Some collection agencies try to take advantage and attempt to do a double collection

*If a collection agency agent lies or uses deceptive language.

NB: Since the use of the term deceptive is quite vague, you can take advantage and get yourself off the hook.

*If a debt collector leaves unclean messages on your answering machine. If they leave such a message, they must state that they are trying to collect debt. They must also leave their name and the name of the agency they are acting for.

*If they sue or threaten to sue after 4 years lapse after you attended to a debt. Note that the duration may differ in CA and a few other states.

*If they threaten and refer to being connected to a government agency courts or any law enforcement agent.

*When they threaten to sue you when they have no intention of doing so.

*If they threaten to garnish your income without explaining the due process. A creditor is supposed to file a suit and obtain judgment before they can garnish the income of debtors.

*If they sue you in another place other than where you live now and where you agreed

All you have to do to start the process is to tell them that you have been recording all their calls.

Conclusion

Having a negative item on your credit report is really a pain in the neck, especially if you are maintaining a good credit standing. If you wish to have these negative items removed, you can always resort to doing it by yourself, or seeking assistance from professional credit repair agencies. The bottom line is, make sure to keep your credit scores up as much and as long as you can. You will never know the benefits that you will get from when the need arises for you to use your credit history as proof of your credit worthiness.

www.ingramcontent.com/pod-product-compliance
Lightning Source LLC
Chambersburg PA
CBHW061021220326
41597CB00016BB/1932